Britain's M

THE OFFICIAL PICTORIAL HISTORY

THE QUEEN MARY

Text by Robert O. Maguglin
Historical Consultant: William M. Winberg

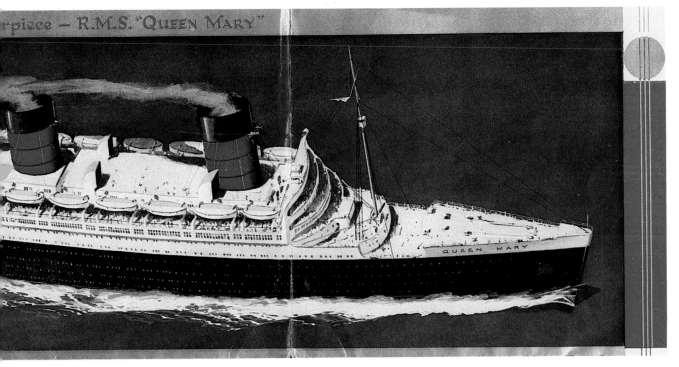

rpiece – R.M.S. "QUEEN MARY"

QUEEN MARY

RMS FOUNDATION, INC., LONG BEACH, CALIFORNIA

Engine telegraph from the ship's bridge is used to send maneuvering commands to the engine room.

A C K N O W L E D G M E N T S

Thank you to the following who made unique contributions to this publication:
Richard Radstone, Alex Marshall, Linda Davis, Nicky Leach, and William Winberg.

Editor: Angela Tripp
Production Manager: Joanne Station
Designer: Mary Schlesinger, Schlesinger Design
Typography: Friedrich Typography and The TypeStudio

Produced by
Albion Publishing Group
Santa Barbara, CA
(805) 963-6004
Lorie Bacon, Publisher

Library of Congress Catalog Number: 91-75773
ISBN 1-880352-07-9

Cunard White Star publicity poster showing the Queen Mary, Aquitania, *and* Berengaria.

P H O T O G R A P H Y

C O N T E N T S

Early artist's rendering of the Queen Mary *showing passengers
lounging and strolling on the proposed liner's spacious Sun Deck.*

Britannia 1840   1,135 tons

Persia 1856   3,300 tons

Bothnia 1874   4,535 tons

CUNARD
125th ANNIVERSARY
1840~1965

Campania 1893   12,950 tons

Mauretania 1907   31,938 tons

Queen Mary 80,774 tons

Queen Elizabeth 83,678 tons

Carmania 22,600 tons

Special Cunard 125th Anniversary menu cover
celebrates a progression of the company's
most famous ships.

B I R T H   O F   T H E
SUPERLINERS

Workmen are dwarfed by one of the ship's massive thirty-five-ton manganese bronze propellers. Each blade is seven feet high, yet the propeller is so perfectly balanced, it can be turned by hand.

Chapter I

The *Queen Mary*, perhaps the most illustrious ship in history, began as a single line on a piece of paper in 1926 as the planning committee of the Cunard Steamship Company contemplated the modernization of its passenger ship fleet.

Cunard was in a precarious position. For decades, the company was at the forefront of the transatlantic steamship trade. But at the close of the 1920s, it began falling behind.

Cunard's prized luxury liner, the *Lusitania*, was sunk at the beginning of World War I and, during the course of the conflict, many other Cunard vessels followed her to the bottom. At the war's end, German, French, Italian, and American shipyards and maritime companies began to challenge Britain's preeminent position on the high seas.

Then, following firmly in the footsteps of the shipping line's legendary founder, Samuel Cunard, the planning committee prepared to take a bold step into the future — a step upon which the company's financial future and that of its thousands of employees depended.

Conferring with the Cunard staff of designers and marine engineers, the company's top executives examined the requirements for modernizing its fleet. They envisioned weekly sailings from New York to Southampton involving two ships instead of the three then required, a reduction that would provide great economic relief through reduced operating, personnel, and fuel costs. To maintain the weekly schedule, however, the two transatlantic liners had to be faster than any existing ship. The minimum cruising speed necessary to stay on schedule was 28½ knots (32.8 MPH/ 52.8 kmph). To achieve this, the vessel had to be larger than any ship then in service in order to house the massive machinery needed to increase its speed.

Shipyard workmen put finishing touches on one of the Queen Mary's *steel masts.*

A thirty-five-ton propeller is a real attention-getter as it leaves the Manganese Bronze & Brass Co., Ltd. factory in Millwall, London, for its journey to Southampton to be fitted on the Queen Mary. *The ship's four propellers were the world's largest.*

Since the first ships sailed the Atlantic Ocean, speed, size, and mechanical complexity of the vessels continually increased. The earliest-known people to cross the mighty Atlantic were the Vikings, who sailed to the New World in rickety longboats. The Scandinavians were followed by other adventurous Europeans who explored the North and South American coasts in small, squat ships.

As colonies became established in North America, Europeans coveted the wealth of the new land, and their need for reliable transportation to cross the Atlantic became a principal concern. Over time, sea-going vessels evolved into efficient sailing packets (mail ships that sailed on regular schedules dictated by the weather and tides).

The epitome of sailing was reached with the advent of clipper ships. Slim, sturdy, and well built, these vessels were able to withstand all but the severest of the ocean's furies. The clippers were swift-sailing ships, but with the vagaries of time and tide, a crossing from England to New York could take thirty days or more. And as strong as the clippers were, many ships still succumbed to the violence of the North Atlantic weather. Passengers sailed out of necessity, not for pleasure, and with the knowledge that they might not survive the crossing. In addition, the rigors of shipboard life were grim. Passengers' quarters were cramped and overcrowded. Food on the long voyage was substandard and, during storms or merely rough seas, no cooking was possible.

But the invention of the steam engine promised a bright future for the transatlantic trade. Ships crossed the Atlantic in the early 1800s using a combination of steam and sails. Then, in April 1938, the *Sirius* steamed from Cork, Ireland, to New York in nineteen days without the aid of its auxiliary sails.

The Queen Mary's *huge cast-steel stern frame takes shape at the Darlington Forge. Weighing 190 tons, it was the largest in the world.*

Job Number 534's size makes workmen appear tiny in comparison. In the foreground, the Second-Class Swimming Pool is taking shape; in the upper portion of the photo, two massive main strong beams mark space for the engine rooms.

This illustration depicts Samuel Cunard's first steamship, the Britannia, *making her way through a narrow channel cut into the ice in Boston Harbor in February 1844. Boston merchants had the 100-foot-wide, seven-mile-long channel cut to allow the Cunarder to use the harbor. The vessel is shown departing for Liverpool.*

Atlantic crossings by steam vessels after the *Sirius*'s successful voyage were numerous yet sporadic. A sailing ship might have to wait weeks for favorable weather or tides before sailing, making it impossible to schedule departures and arrivals.

Samuel Cunard, in his effort to standardize the occasional adventurous crossings of the Atlantic, saw the steamships as the means of achieving a great purpose. He realized that a reliable steamship service could be very profitable, especially in the transportation of mail between the continents.

In 1838 the British government invited bids from commercial companies to carry mail across the Atlantic, and Cunard formed the British and North American Royal Mail Steam Packet Company, later renamed the Cunard Steamship Company. He ordered his first ship, the *Britannia*, from a Scottish shipbuilding firm. She had paddle wheels amidships on either side of her hull, was 207 feet long, weighed 1,154 tons, and could carry 225 tons of cargo and 115 passengers at a contract speed of 9 knots (10.4 MPH/16.7 kmph).

The *Britannia* set sail on her maiden voyage from Liverpool to Boston via Halifax on July 4, 1840. She arrived in Halifax in 12 days and 10 hours with an average speed of 8 knots (9.2 MPH/14.8 kmph) for the 3,000-mile crossing. The *Britannia* was soon followed by her sister ships, the new Cunarders *Acadia, Caledonia,* and *Columbia.* From this small beginning, Samuel Cunard built the company that eventually reaped the lion's share of the transatlantic passenger trade.

It was not long before marine designers planned larger vessels with greater speed, in an attempt to use three ships instead of four to maintain weekly crossings of the Atlantic. The technological advancements made in transatlantic vessels were rapid in the Cunard Steamship Company. The wooden hull gave way to iron in 1852 with the *Andes,* and the paddle wheel was superseded by the screw propeller in 1862 with the *China.* Passenger accommodations became more comfortable and, in the 1870s,

One of the Queen Mary's *sixteen turbine rotors. Each of the ship's 257,000 turbine blades was individually set by hand to ensure perfect alignment.*

the first ships with private bathrooms and promenade decks, upon which passengers could stroll and relax, were launched. Steel hulls replaced iron in 1881 with the *Servia*, the first Cunarder to be illuminated with electric lights. Twin propellers debuted on the liners *Campania* and *Lucania*. Steam turbine machinery replaced reciprocating engines in 1905 with the *Carmania*. Each new generation of steamship was larger, faster, and more comfortable than the last.

The financial reward of owning the swiftest ship could not be ignored. Passengers wanted to travel on the fleetest ships, and the vessel holding the record for the fastest crossing was always in great demand.

After World War I, with the *Mauretania, Aquitania,* and *Berengaria* (formerly the *Imperator*), Cunard implemented a three-ship service providing weekly sailings between New York and England, made possible by the twenty-two to twenty-five-knot service speeds (25.3 to 28.8 MPH/ 40.7 to 46.3 kmph) of these three ships. When coal gave way to oil-fired boilers in 1920, marine technology reached a stage where the ultimate goal of a two-ship service became feasible. And in 1926, the planning committee of the Cunard Steamship Company was ready to make the goal a reality.

Although the ship eventually became one of the fastest and largest vessels ever built, it was initially designed as the "slowest and smallest" ship capable of maintaining an average cruising speed of 28½ knots, and of adequate size to carry enough cargo and passengers to pay its operational costs. The final plans called for a total length of 1,019½ feet and a gross tonnage of 80,774 — nearly twice the size of the ill-fated *Titanic*.

It was soon apparent that the liner's size created problems. Nothing so large had ever been built, and the design taxed the skill and craftsmanship of both the designers and the builders. An adequate dry dock did not exist, nor was a launching facility available. More importantly, existing docking facilities on both sides of the Atlantic were not capable of handling a ship of that size.

But one by one the problems were solved. The Southern Railways Company agreed to construct a huge stationary dry dock in Southampton, and New York and Southampton port authorities consented to build facilities to accommodate the giant liner.

Workmen use a giant-sized chain in preparation for lifting the huge stern frame weighing 190 tons.

Sparks fly at Beardmore Parkhead Forge in Glasgow as a workman prepares castings for the new Cunarder.

With these major obstacles removed, serious planning began on the new ship. For two years, naval architects and planners worked out the details of construction. Thousands of tank tests were conducted to determine the vessel's hull shape and propeller design. Wind tunnel tests were performed to ensure that the ship's funnels properly carried smoke and fumes away from the passenger decks. Comparisons were made, and the most efficient propulsion system for the giant liner was carefully chosen.

Cunard's *Mauretania*, which held the transatlantic speed record with the *Lusitania* for a combined twenty-two years, was a steam turbine vessel with coal-fired boilers that were later converted to oil-fired boilers. But advances in both turbo-electric and diesel engines interested the Cunard designers. They finally decided that steam turbine engines using a single reduction gear would provide the best engine performance. The single reduction gear allowed the turbines to spin at high speeds while the propellers revolved at slow speeds, at which the two pieces of machinery were most efficient.

Job Number 534 serves as a mute symbol of modern-day technology, contrasting sharply with the rural farmer across the Clyde River, cutting his crop with a Clydesdale-horse-drawn reaper.

Finally, in December 1930, the first rivet was ceremoniously placed in the longest keel ever laid in a British shipyard. John Brown & Company, Clydebank, Scotland, was chosen by Cunard to build Job Number 534, the only designation the ship carried until her christening and launch.

The ship's hull soon rose high over the shipyard, and sightseers on the Clyde River marveled at the enormous steel behemoth taking shape before their eyes.

But one year after construction began, disaster struck. The Great Depression hit England hard, and Cunard found itself in financial difficulty. Drastic cost-cutting measures were adopted, but they were not enough. The banks refused to lend Cunard the funds necessary to finish the great liner. All work on Job Number 534 came to an abrupt halt on December 10, 1931.

The winter was bleak for the Clydebank workmen and their families. One observer wrote, "the great vessel — no longer reverberating to the rhythm of the hammers — lay silent, a symbol of the cold hand of economic stress which lay on the hearts of the people." Thousands of jobs were lost all over Great Britain when shops and factories fabricating or preparing to fabricate parts, fixtures, and accessories for the new ship were forced to cancel production and lay off employees.

For more than two years, the ship's unfinished hull towered above the quiet shipyard, a stark symbol of the grim hardship that held the people of Great Britain in its grip. During these years, other governments stepped in to aid their shipbuilding and maritime industries. France's government subsidized the continuing construction of the liner *Normandie*, while in Great Britain, the issue of government assistance for Job Number 534 was cautiously debated in Parliament. But not until 1934 was a satisfactory agreement reached.

The British government agreed to finance Job Number 534 and her sister ship, but required that Cunard merge with England's other great transatlantic shipping line, White Star. Early in 1934, the two companies became the Cunard White Star Line and, on April 3, 1934, work resumed on Job Number 534. It was a joyous day for all of Great Britain, but especially for the Clydebank workers and their families. The men marched lightheartedly back into the shipyard, led by bagpipers and cheered by hundreds of the town's residents.

Work resumed on Job Number 534 in April 1934, after a lapse of nearly three years due to the Great Depression. It was a joyous occasion for all Clydeside residents, most of whom depended upon the shipyard for their livelihood. The liner's hull towers over the village streets as the "Clydesiders" march proudly back to work.

Number 534

Dockworkers handle the Queen Mary's heavy hawsers as the ship is maneuvered into Southampton's King George V dry dock.

One of the vessel's 40,000-horsepower steam turbine engines is tested in the John Brown & Company engineering shop before being taken apart and reassembled in the Queen Mary's hull.

For ages you were rock, far below light,
Crushed, without shape, the earth's unregarded bone.
Then Man in all the marvel of his might
Quarried you out and burned you from the stone.

Then, being pured to essence, you were nought
But weight and hardness, body without nerve;
Then Man in all the marvel of his thought,
Smithied you into form of leap and curve;

And took you, so, and bent you to his vast,
Intense great world of passionate design,
Curve after changing curving, braced and masst
To stand all tumult that can tumble brine,

And left you, this, a rampart of a ship,
Long as a street and lofty as a tower,
Ready to glide in thunder from the slip
And shear the sea with majesty of power.

I long to see you leaping to the urge
Of the great engines, rolling as you go,
Parting the seas in sunder in a surge,
Shredding a trackway like a mile of snow

With all the wester streaming from your hull
And all gear twanging shrilly as you race,
And effortless above your stern a gull
Leaning upon the blast and keeping place.

May shipwreck and collision, fog and fire,
Rock, shoal and other evils of the sea,
Be kept from you; and may the heart's desire
Of those who speed your launching come to be.

John Masefield

To commemorate the launch of Great Britain's greatest liner, British Poet Laureate John Masefield wrote this special poem, appropriately entitled Number 534.

The Secret of a Name

When the time came to launch the partially completed hull and christen it with a name, all of Great Britain held its collective breath. The company had kept the name for the new ship a closely guarded secret. Many thought Cunard would continue its tradition of choosing names ending in "-ia" (as in *Lusitania* and *Mauretania*), while others believed the name would end in "-ic" (as did White Star's *Titanic* and *Olympic*, for example). Some astute observers predicted that, to accommodate the consolidation of the two shipping lines, the new ship's name would be the first of an entirely new style. Interest in the naming of Job Number 534 became intense. Although the subject of widespread newpaper and radio speculation, the Cunarder's name remained secret until the official christening.

September 26, 1934, dawned with cold winds and heavily overcast skies. Rain fell intermittently throughout the day. At the John Brown & Company shipyard, thousands of spectators huddled together, shivering in the biting cold. Every inch of available space was occupied by an estimated 200,000 curious Britons, anxious to witness the launch of the greatest vessel ever built. On the Clyde River, boats were jammed with additional sightseers. For every Briton, the new Cunarder was special. It was their ship, the pride of British art and craftsmanship and a symbol of the indomitable spirit of a nation recovering from economic ruin — the ship they hoped would reclaim Great Britain's place of honor on the North Atlantic.

Soon, the secret of the new liner's name would be revealed. On hand to perform this historic christening was Her Majesty Queen Mary. For the first time in Great Britain's history, a reigning queen was to christen a merchant vessel, an unprecedented occasion. But no one foresaw the actual significance of Her Majesty's participation.

During the prelaunch ceremonies, King George V spoke to the crowd. His speech was short but effective, closing with the words, "Today we can send her forth no longer a number on the books, but a ship with a name . . . alive with beauty, energy and strength . . . the stateliest ship now in being. . . ."

Then, Her Majesty Queen Mary stepped forward to the microphone. A hush of expectancy fell over the crowd. With nervous dignity, the queen gently snipped the satin cord holding a bottle of Australian white wine, sending it crashing against the bow plates of Job Number 534. As the bottle shattered, she pressed a small button to fire the launch triggers, and her voice rang out, "I am happy to name this ship the *Queen Mary*. I wish success to her and to all who sail in her."

The crowd exploded with a roar of approval. No finer name could have been chosen for Great Britain's new Monarch of the Seas than that of their beloved Queen Mary — the first time in history that a merchant vessel bore the name of a reigning queen.

With the words "I am happy to name this ship the Queen Mary. *I wish success to her and to all who sail in her," Her Majesty Queen Mary pressed a button that sent the massive hull sliding down the ways and into the waters of the Clyde River.*

Ornate ceremonial scissors used to snip the ribbon that sent a bottle of Australian white wine crashing against the bow plates of the newest and largest Cunard liner during the christening ceremony. These same scissors were later used at the launching ceremonies of the Queen Elizabeth *and the* QE2.

THIS CASKET WAS WROUGHT FOR HER MAJESTY, QUEEN MARY, BY COMMAND OF JOHN BROWN & COMPANY TO MARK THE OCCASION OF

THE LARGEST VESSEL THAT EVER TOOK THE WATER

LEIF ERIKSSON Circa 900 AD

The MAYFLOWER 1620

The SANTA MARIA 1492

HER MAJESTY'S GRACIOUS ACT *in* LAUNCHING *at their* CLYDEBANK SHIPYARD *on* SEPTEMBER 26th 1934 *The* CUNARD WHITE STAR EXPRESS LINER No 534

Lid of a special commemorative chest presented to Her Majesty Queen Mary by the John Brown & Company shipyard. The lovely chest is hand-wrought of chiseled steel and mounted in gold and silver plate.

King George V and Queen Mary greet thousands of spectators who throng into the John Brown & Company shipyard to watch the new liner's launch.

LAUNCH OF
the
"QUEEN MARY"
in the presence of Their Majesties
THE KING & QUEEN
Wednesday, September 26, 1934
at Clydebank

The medallion found on the cover of a booklet commemorating the launch of the ship, printed after the ceremonies.

Ready for launch, the awe-inspiring hull of Job Number 534 looms over the shipyard. Cribbing blocks have been placed beneath the hull, and tons of tallow grease the slipway.

For decades, a legend has surrounded the naming of the *Queen Mary*. Finally the true account has come from the daughter of Sir Ashley Sparks, then chairman of Cunard Line in America. She explains, "My father was part of a small delegation from Cunard Line that called on King George V to ask his permission to name their new superliner after Queen Victoria." (Traditionally, Cunard ships had names that ended with "ia" and Victoria would have been an excellent choice.)

She continues, "My father opened the conversation with His Majesty by saying . . . that Cunard wished to name its new superliner 'after England's greatest queen.' Queen Mary, who was with her husband on this occasion, smiled and said, 'I would be delighted.'" And so the new vessel was named the RMS *Queen Mary*.

The launch button the queen had pressed fired small electrically released triggers holding the massive hull in place on the launch ways. For twenty-four seconds, nothing seemed to happen; then, with a low groan that rose quickly in intensity, the mammoth hull slid toward the water of the Clyde River. As the vessel moved down the ways, 2,300 tons of drag chains unraveled to slow the ship's momentum. When the hull hit the water, it sent a two-foot wave across the Clyde to lap over the feet of spectators crowding the riverbank. The entire launch took just 112 seconds, one second longer than engineers predicted.

The ship was afloat, dwarfing the tugboats rushing in to shepherd the enormous hull to dockside, where it was tied up. With the launch successfully accomplished, work resumed to finish the ship. Her huge boilers and engines were installed, and the superstructure was completed.

Afloat! With a mighty groan, the massive ship, now officially named the Queen Mary, *slides gracefully into the waters of the Clyde River. More than 2,000 tons of drag chains (attached to the ship's hull) slow, then stop, the ship's momentum. A two-foot wave splashes spectators on the opposite side of the river.*

This new vessel was ultimately known as "the inevitable ship." Hundreds of years of progress and experience in the art and craft of shipbuilding converged with the *Queen Mary*. When the ship sailed on her maiden voyage in 1936, twenty months after her launch, she was the ultimate passenger vessel. In later years, more modern ships were built — two liners were larger and one was faster — but the *Queen Mary* represented the high-water mark in transatlantic travel.

The Queen Mary's *first captain, Commodore Sir Edgar Britten, inspects one of the ship's sixteen-ton anchors.*

21

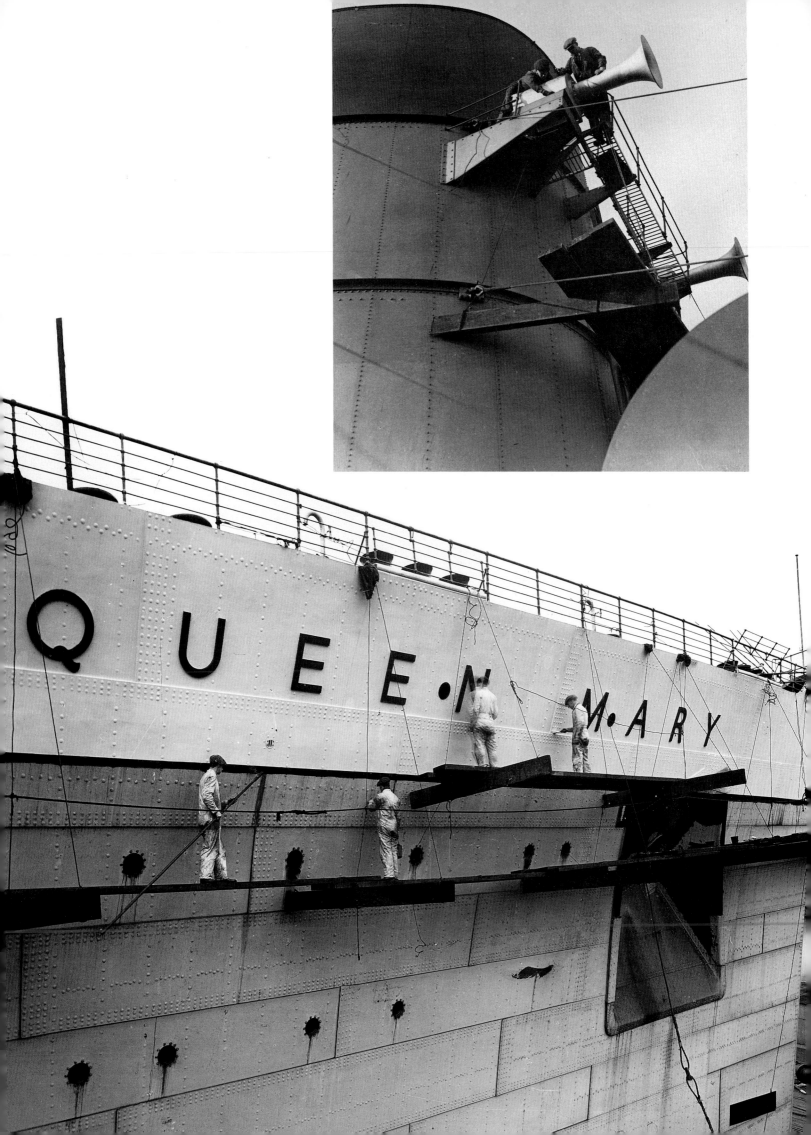

Opposite page:
Workmen install two of the ship's three whistles.
Each whistle weighs one ton and is seven feet long.
Tuned to lower bass "A," the whistles can be heard
for ten miles at sea.

After launching, work continues on the ship's upper
superstructure. The lifeboat davits form a canopy
down the length of the Sun Deck.

Shipyard workmen leave the Queen
Mary *at the end of a workday.*

Opposite page:
Painters put finishing touches on the Queen Mary's *paint job.*
Each letter in the ship's name is two-and-a-half feet high; the
entire name stretches for more than fifty-five feet.

Girls from the Queen Mary School in Lytham present the Queen Mary's captain, Sir Edgar Britten, with a special blue ensign. The flag, sewn by the girls especially for the ship, was flown on the maiden voyage.

Noted British artist Edward Wadsworth at work on his painting, Dressed Overall at the Quay, *in the First-Class Smoking Lounge.*

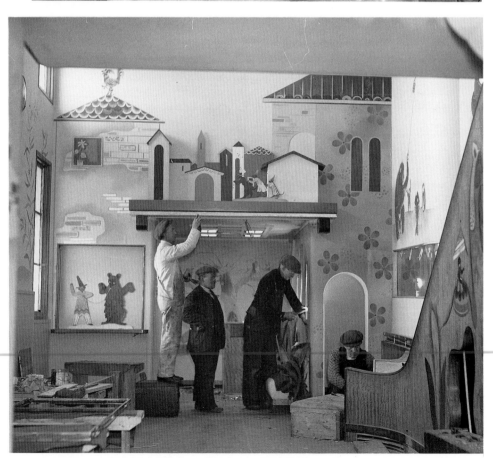

A fantasy land for children. Workmen install play equipment and artwork in the First-Class Children's Playroom, which even had a full-size slide (at right). Princess Elizabeth (later Queen Elizabeth II) was the first to zoom down the slide.

The Observation Lounge still functions today. Inserts show the colorful characters featured in the painting The Royal Jubilee Week, 1935 *by A. R. Thompson, depicting the celebration of King George V's twenty-fifth year as king.*

Workers install fixtures (lower photo) in the Observation Lounge, destined to become one of the most popular public rooms on the Queen Mary. *Marvelously decorated in a pleasing array of art deco schemes, the bar offered a breathtaking view of the sea over the ship's bow.*

This cast likeness of Her Majesty Queen Mary hangs in a place of honor over the main staircase on the Promenade Deck.

A map of the North Atlantic from the First-Class Dining Salon. Passengers could follow the ship's course as a crystal ship moved across the map.

Down River to the Sea

On March 24, 1936 the *Queen Mary* was ready to leave the shipyard. Tugboats gently nudged the giant liner into the narrow channel of the Clyde River, parts of which were widened to allow the ship's passage. Once in midchannel, the *Queen Mary*'s massive propellers began to move the ship down river. Vigilant tugboats stayed alongside to maneuver the ship around the river's tight turns. Still, the *Queen Mary* ran aground twice. Fortunately, the ship was not damaged, and the flotilla of tugboats pulled her free. After completing her sea trials, the *Queen Mary* steamed to Southampton to begin final preparation for her maiden voyage scheduled May 27, 1936 — just one day after the sixty-ninth birthday of Her Majesty Queen Mary.

The Queen Mary's First-Class Dining Salon, now called the Grand Salon, is the largest room ever built on a passenger ship. It is three decks high, 143 feet long, and 118 feet wide (the entire width of the liner). The room, with its foyer, is so large that it can accommodate Cunard's first ship, the Britannia, plus Columbus's Nina, Pinta, and Santa Maria.

As the Queen Mary was maneuvered down the Clyde River en route from the shipyard to open sea, a gust of wind caught the liner. Before the captain or crew could react, the huge ship turned broadside in the river. Her stern went aground and tugboats rushed in, quickly pulling the Queen Mary to safety.

An early rendering shows the magnificent elegance and incredible size of the new liner's Main Lounge. This room was the primary social center for the Queen Mary's First-Class passengers.

QUEEN MARY:

THE PRIDE
OF GREAT BRITAIN

The Queen Mary kicks up a wake during maneuvering trials off the Isle of Arran in April 1936. In this photo, the Queen Mary has a "bone in her teeth," a nautical expression used to describe the white water frothing high on her bow, a clear indication of a vessel steaming at high speed.

Chapter 1

The Cunard Line House Flag with its proud gold lion, flown throughout the Queen Mary's peacetime career.

On May 25, 1936, King Edward VIII and his royal party arrived at the Ocean Dock in Southampton to visit the *Queen Mary*. With him were the Duke and Duchess of York (later King George VI and Queen Elizabeth), their daughter Princess Elizabeth (later Queen Elizabeth II), the Duke and Duchess of Kent, the Duchess of Gloucester, and the most honored member of the royal party, Queen Mary, who was seeing the ship for the first time since christening her.

Two days later, the massive seven-foot whistles of the *Queen Mary* shattered the air with mighty blasts, signaling the beginning of the ship's first passenger voyage. On board were 1,742 passengers — 708 First Class, 631 Second Class, and 403 Third Class — and a crew of 1,186 men and women.

A remarkable cutaway drawing shows the amazing diversity and conplexity of the Queen Mary's *passenger and engine compartments.*

A close-up of some of the intricate glasswork from the Verandah Grill.

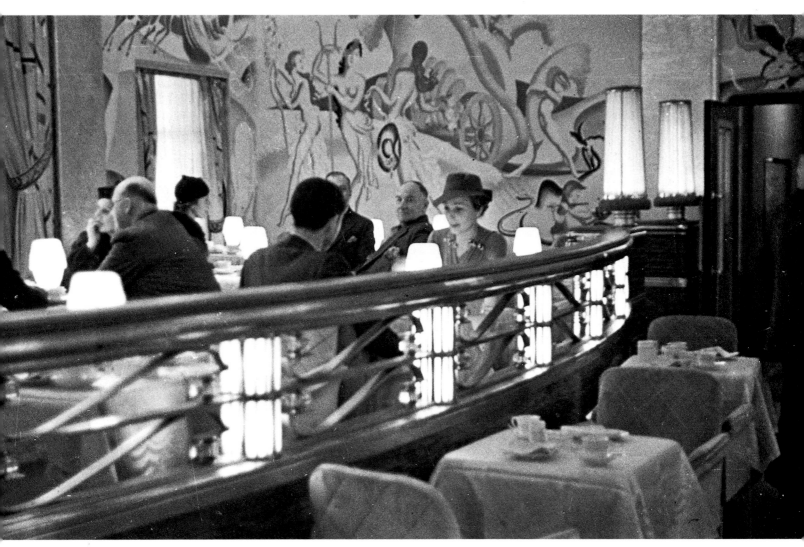

Top: A re-creation of the Verandah Grill, the Queen Mary's *most exclusive dining room and nightspot. Usually, tables had to be reserved months in advance of sailing. While all meals were included in the price of passage, dining in the Verandah Grill was an extra charge.*

Bottom: Passengers enjoy an evening of music and conversation in the ship's First-Class Ballroom.

The people of Great Britain had waited ten years for this day, and they made the most of it. Nothing was too good for their country's prize liner. Thousands of cheering spectators lined the docks, while hundreds of small boats — from paddle steamers to row boats — bobbed along in the *Queen Mary*'s wake as she slowly made her way toward the open sea. Overhead, circling airplanes carried reporters and photographers. On the dock, the Royal Marine Corps Band played "Rule Britannia" as six tugboats assisted the giant ship on her way.

The blue ensign was hoisted up the mainmast, signifying that the *Queen Mary*'s captain, Commodore Sir Edgar Britten, was a Royal Naval Reserve officer. Signaling the tugboats with a blast of her whistles, the *Queen Mary* steamed up Southampton water and moved majestically toward the open sea.

On board for the maiden voyage were more than 100 reporters and newspapermen. The British Broadcasting Corporation had installed twenty-three remote microphones throughout the ship, and during the voyage, twenty broadcasters from five countries conducted live broadcasts from locations such as the engine rooms, bridge, and Main Lounge. Interest in the *Queen Mary* extended across the Atlantic as well — two American companies had also sent teams of radio newsmen to record the historic maiden voyage.

The ship's crew loaded 6,124 sacks of mail bound for the United States and Canada. All over the world, stamp collectors eyed the coveted cancellation "Posted at sea, via RMS *Queen Mary* Maiden Voyage, May 27, 1936."

On B Deck, the *Queen Mary*'s three telephone operators prepared for the expected barrage of phone calls as soon as the ship cleared port. The

The Hales Trophy was presented to the ship with the fastest North Atlantic round-trip crossing time. Originated by Harold K. Hales, a member of British Parliament, the trophy was administered by an international committee headed by the Duke of Sutherland. Although the Queen Mary *held the speed record for fourteen years, Cunard refused to accept the Hales Trophy. It was Cunard's policy not to resort to speed for speed's sake. The company insisted that the* Queen Mary's *record crossings were to provide data for future ship designs.*

Queen Mary had 600 telephone receivers, one in every First-Class cabin and dozens in other locations available to all passengers. The first ship to have a sophisticated ship-to-shore radiotelephone system, the *Queen Mary* not only allowed passengers to ring each other cabin-to-cabin, but also anywhere in the world they called home, even while in mid-Atlantic.

Upon leaving Southampton, the *Queen Mary* sailed across the channel to Cherbourg, France, to embark an additional 107 passengers and mail. In Cherbourg the *Queen Mary*'s first stowaway, a Canadian woman journalist who decried the exclusion of women reporters on the ship's maiden voyage and decided to stow away as a bid for publicity, quietly disembarked before the ship sailed for New York. Later, her adventure was reported in newspapers around the world.

During the crossing, the *Queen Mary*'s second stowaway was discovered: forty-one-year-old Frank Gardner, an unemployed laborer from Cardiff. He walked aboard posing as a greaser and hid in the number one cargo hold. Gardner was put to work during the voyage helping the kitchen staff, but once the *Queen Mary* reached New York, he was promptly arrested and shipped back to England.

The Blue Riband

People on both sides of the Atlantic waited breathlessly to see if the *Queen Mary* would break the transatlantic speed record held by France's *Normandie*. Cunard traditionally denied the company was interested in speed records — eventually insisting that the *Queen Mary*'s record-breaking crossing was mainly a trial run for her soon-to-be-built sister ship — but they knew a ship's speed had a direct effect on its profits since passengers flocked to the fleetest liner. So intense was the competition to be the fastest, that an unofficial but highly coveted prize was created: the Blue Riband, symbolized by the exquisitely crafted solid-silver trophy donated in 1935 by British Member of Parliament Harold Hales. The ship capturing the prize garnered tremendous prestige.

Captain Sir Edgar Britten (third from left) and Chief Engineer Llewellyn Roberts (second from right) are greeted by Southampton dignitaries after the Queen Mary's *record-breaking run in August 1936. The liner crossed the North Atlantic in under four days, the first ship ever to do so.*

The Queen Mary's *captain, Sir Edgar Britten, on the bridge during the ship's maiden voyage.*

Cunard held the distinction of owning the fastest ships from 1907 to 1929. During those twenty-two years, the *Mauretania* and *Lusitania* maintained the crossing records. But the German liner *Bremen* captured the record from the aging *Mauretania* in 1929, passing it to her sister ship, the *Europa*, in 1930. The Italian liner *Rex* set the record in 1933 and held it until 1935, when the *Normandie* captured it on her maiden voyage.

The much asked question was, "Would the *Queen Mary* recapture the Blue Riband for Great Britain, and could she do it on her maiden voyage?" Unfortunately, the *Queen Mary* was slowed by fog, and did not make a record crossing. As far back as 1840, Samuel Cunard issued standing orders to the captains of his ships that "In any case when, in sailing, you are overtaken by thick weather, the most extreme caution is to be exercised and you are not to be actuated by any desire to complete the voyage on schedule, your sole consideration being the safety of your ship."

The *Queen Mary*'s inability to break the speed record on her maiden voyage did not diminish New York City's gala reception for Great Britain's newest superliner. New Yorkers turned out by the tens of thousands to greet the *Queen Mary* as she glided past the Statue of Liberty and up the Hudson River. Hundreds of boats crowded with enthusiastic spectators trailed in the great ship's wake.

Overhead, airplanes swooped and circled around the *Queen Mary*. Several hours before, as she approached the New York coast from the open sea, a DC-2 piloted by famed World War I ace Eddie Rickenbacker flew to greet the ship. Aboard the plane were newsmen and press photographers, anxious for the first view and first photos of the *Queen Mary* at sea. The trim twin-engine aircraft flew low over the huge liner, dropping thousands of white carnations on her decks in greeting. As the *Queen Mary* sailed majestically up the Hudson, with the skyscrapers of Manhattan as a backdrop and her decks showered with snowy carnations, she looked every inch a queen.

Occasionally, one of the larger excursion steamers pulled close alongside the liner while a band on its upper decks played a musical salute. On the *Queen Mary*'s open Sun Deck, Musical Director Henry Hall conducted the ship's band as it replied with her own signature tune, "Somewhere at Sea," that he had written especially for the great vessel.

First voyage! A flotilla of boats escorting the RMS Queen Mary *as she departs from her Southampton berth on her maiden voyage, May 27, 1936.*

A small flotilla of tugboats gently nudged the *Queen Mary* into her berth at Pier 90 on the Hudson River. After a special dockside arrival ceremony, Captain Britten and Cunard Chairman Sir Percy Bates led a delegation of Cunard officials to City Hall for a formal welcoming ceremony, where they were greeted by Mayor Fiorello La Guardia. Representing the royal family were the Marquis and Marchioness of Milford Haven.

Curious New Yorkers were allowed aboard the *Queen Mary* while she was in New York Harbor for a fee of $1 each, which was donated to the seamen's relief fund. Thousands descended upon the *Queen Mary*. Souvenir hunters pocketed anything that was removeable — ashtrays, silverware, brass hardware, plants, and even teapots.

First-Class passengers play deck games on the Sports Deck, the highest passenger deck on the ship.

Three months after the maiden voyage, in August 1936, the *Queen Mary* captured the Blue Riband from the *Normandie*, officially completing the Atlantic crossing in 3 days, 23 hours, and 57 minutes from Ambrose Lightship outside New York Harbor to Bishop Rock off the western tip of England. The *Queen Mary*'s average speed was 30.63 knots for the nearly 3,000-mile crossing. More than 35 miles per hour (56.73 kmph), it was an incredible speed for a ship grossing more than 80,000 tons.

In order to claim the Blue Riband, a ship had to post the fastest time both ways on the transatlantic route. Since she completed her Southampton-to-New York run in 4 days and 27 minutes at an average speed of 30.14 knots (34.69 MPH/55.82 kmph), the *Queen Mary* surpassed the *Normandie*'s best time by 2 hours and 35 minutes.

As the *Queen Mary* sailed up Southampton water, thousands of cheering spectators, alerted by radio of the new record, turned out to cheer. Dozens of steamers, yachts, and pleasure craft turned out to toot their whistles as they followed the *Queen Mary* to her berth.

But the *Queen Mary* only briefly held the record. The following year, the *Normandie* posted a westbound crossing of 3 days, 23 hours, and 2 minutes at an average speed of 30.58 knots (35.19 MPH/56.64 kmph), and an eastbound time of 3 days, 22 hours, and 7 minutes at an average speed of 31.2 knots (35.9 MPH/57.5 kmph).

Cunard's engineers reviewed the *Queen Mary*'s design and decided her performance could be improved with a new type of propeller. A set of thirty-ton, four-bladed propellers was cast of manganese bronze. Each propeller was eighteen feet in diameter. The *Queen Mary*, with her new propellers installed, finally settled her rivalry with the *Normandie* in August 1938. She steamed to New York in 3 days, 21 hours, and 48 minutes at an average speed of 30.99 knots (35.66 MPH/57.39 kmph), and returned to England even faster in 3 days, 20 hours, and 42 minutes at an average speed of 31.69 knots (36.47 MPH/58.67 kmph). The *Queen Mary* had set a new speed record, which she held for the next fourteen years. Not until 1952 was her record defeated, and then by the SS *United States*, a much lighter ship that benefitted from great advances in postwar technology.

Passengers gather on the Queen Mary's stern to watch crowded pleasure steamers follow the liner as she departs for Cherbourg on the first leg of her maiden voyage.

A regal Queen Mary passes the Manhattan skyline at the conclusion of her successful maiden voyage on June 1, 1936. Thousands of steamers and pleasure craft turned out to greet the new Queen of the Atlantic.

Bellboys taking passengers' dogs for a walk. The Queen Mary *boasted a full-service kennel, complete with lamppost.*

Service—a Cunard Tradition

The *Queen Mary*'s First-Class passengers traveled with the assurance that every possible convenience and luxury was available to satisfy their every whim. They could relax and enjoy being pampered and entertained.

Personal service was one of the elements that made the *Queen Mary* a great ship. Stewards and stewardesses were carefully chosen by Cunard, some carrying on a tradition begun by their parents or grandparents, and precisely trained to cater to passengers' needs and demands. The bedroom staff took pride in remembering the likes and dislikes of frequent passengers so that all their wishes could be anticipated on subsequent voyages. Anticipation was, in fact, a key word in the ship's philosophy of service. The crew was drilled constantly to anticipate passengers' needs and fulfill them without having to be asked.

Dining aboard the *Queen Mary* was more than just a meal. It was an event — a ritual of culinary elegance. The *Queen Mary*'s cuisine ranked with the very best in the world. Cunard sent its chefs to top restaurants for rigorous training before they were assigned to an ocean liner, where they were expected to be masters of all types of meal preparation. Most, if not all, dishes were included in the chefs' epicurean repertoire. In fact, so sure was the master chef of his ability that he wagered he could prepare anything a passenger might possibly order.

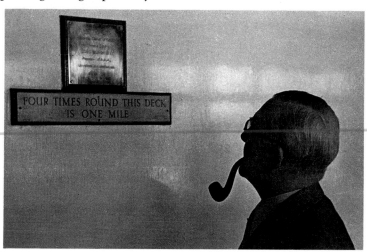

A regular Queen Mary *passenger, Hubert Noble, contemplates a walk around the Promenade Deck.*

When a wealthy Greek asked for couscous, the chef prepared such a delectable steamed wheat-and-lamb stew that he won Grecian accolades from the delighted woman. Southerners from the United States ordered hominy grits for breakfast and enjoyed chicken-fried steak for dinner. The most finicky French gourmet was confident that his discriminating palate would taste French delicacies of incomparable quality.

On only one occasion did the *Queen Mary*'s chef find himself unable to comply exactly with a diner's request. A Texas oilman jokingly ordered "rattlesnake steak," knowing he would certainly stump the chef. Not to be outdone, the chef served the American two baked eels while waiters shook baby rattles over them. Not exactly what the man requested, but certainly a wager-saving substitute.

The evening meal in First Class was a seven-course dinner with all 800 First-Class passengers served in the Dining Salon at one sitting. This event was possible because the *Queen Mary*'s Dining Salon was the largest room ever built within in a ship. Measuring 143 feet by 118 feet, the First-Class Dining Salon was so extensive that Cunard's first steamship, the *Britannia*, could have been placed in the room with Christopher Columbus's *Nina*, *Pinta*, and *Santa Maria* tucked alongside.

Tea time. Passengers lounging on the Promenade Deck are served traditional English tea cakes.

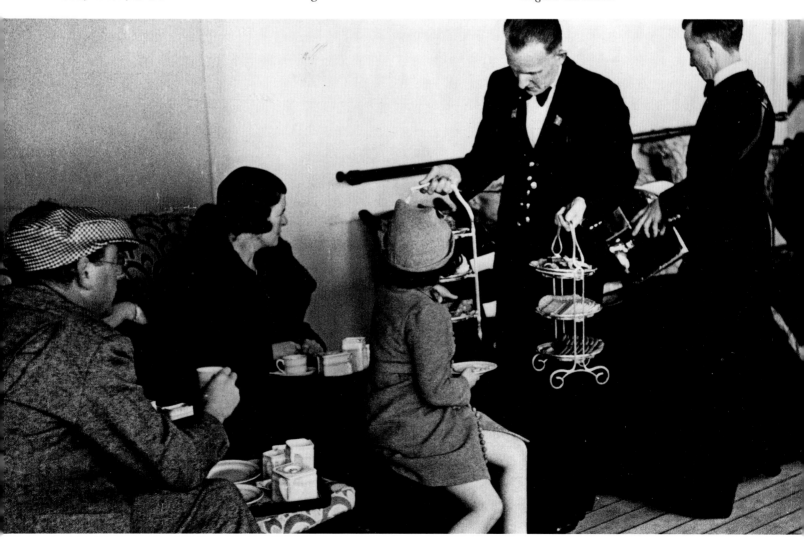

Ship's bellboys line up for a group photograph.

Inspecting some of the Queen Mary's
200,000 pieces of china and glassware.
During rough seas, thousands of pieces
were broken and had to be replaced
from supplies in Southampton.

Although several private dining rooms were available, most passengers preferred the Dining Salon where they could "see and be seen." The world's most famous celebrities dined here — Fred Astaire, Greta Garbo, Bob Hope, Gloria Swanson, Elizabeth Taylor, and Clark Gable. The Baron and Baroness de Rothschild, the Duke and Duchess of Windsor, and the Vanderbilts all praised the *Queen Mary*'s cuisine.

But the most prestigious seats in the *Queen Mary*'s Dining Salon were at the captain's table. Seven auspicious passengers were chosen at the beginning of each crossing to dine with the captain at his table in the center of the Dining Salon. These guests were selected by the captain himself, with company officials proffering names of VIPs who were aboard.

On one of the ship's voyages, the captain had filled all but one place at his table. He glanced at the passenger list. Not recognizing any names, the captain decided to invite the person booked in the ship's most expensive First-Class suite, assuming the man was a prominent figure. He was

A 1936 rendering illustrates the vast
amount of foodstuffs carried on the
Queen Mary for a single voyage.

The ship's stores are loaded aboard by crane. The normal turnaround for the Queen Mary *was twenty-four hours in New York and forty-eight hours in Southampton. In this time, arriving passengers would disembark, departing passengers would board, and all stores, water, and fuel would be loaded – an incredible feat for so short a time.*

actually a Welsh coal miner who had spent his life's savings to take a "dream vacation" aboard the *Queen Mary*, a ship he had loved and admired for many years.

The captain's steward presented the coal miner with the gilt-edged invitation to dine with the captain. Unaware of its significance, he angrily told the steward, "I've saved my entire life for this cruise, and I'll be blasted if I'll spend it eating with the crew!" Once the honor was explained to him, he cheerfully dined with the captain and his other guests, and his voyage became an experience of a lifetime.

To provide enough food for approximately 2,000 passengers and 1,200 crew members, an incredible amount of provisions was loaded aboard the *Queen Mary* before each crossing. The list called for 77,000 pounds of fresh meat, 27,500 pounds of poultry, 11,000 pounds of fresh fish, 50,000 pounds of potatoes, 33,000 pounds of fresh vegetables, 5,000 dozen eggs, 22,000 pounds of flour, 11,000 pounds of sugar, 14,500 gallons of milk, 1,110 boxes of assorted fresh fruit, and 3,000 quarts of ice cream. In addition, the ship's wine cellar contained more than 15,000 bottles of spirits and fine wine, rivaling the cellars of Europe's finest restaurants.

The *Queen Mary*'s First-Class Dining Salon was comparable to the world's best restaurants, but some passengers preferred more exclusive dining. For those discriminating few, the *Queen Mary* offered the Verandah Grill, a small restaurant on the ship's aft Sun Deck. The most exclusive room on the ship, the Verandah Grill seated only eighty-two First-Class passengers at thirty-two tables. Reservations were a must, since an empty seat was rare for dinner, and in most cases, had to be made months in advance.

Queen Elizabeth, wife of King George VI, tours the crew's working alleyway in the Queen Mary.

The Verandah Grill was intended for special a la carte meals during lunch and dinner, and it had its own private bar and kitchen. For the distinction of dining in the Verandah Grill, a patron was charged a £1 cover charge in addition to the price of the meal. At midnight, the tables were removed and the Verandah Grill became the "Starlight Roof" nightclub, offering entertainment and dancing until dawn.

Decorated by Doris Zinkeisen, a well-known British theatrical film costume and set designer of the 1930s, the Verandah Grill featured etched glass panels portraying various musical instruments. The panels, with concealed lights illuminating the edges, decorated the curved center of an elaborate balustrade separating the raised floor from the lower dance floor. Plush burgundy drapes adorned with stitched five-point white stars were drawn back from the tall vertical windows by sashes. The room's jet black carpet created quite a controversy when it was installed. Cunard's management thought it was too "modish," but the carpet became quite a conversation piece.

Onyx fireplace with its Napoleon marble hearth in the First-Class Drawing Room on the Promenade Deck. The large mural over the fireplace, Flower Market, was painted by Kenneth Shoesmith, ROI.

Rabbi uses yud to point to breastplates protecting sections of the Torah used in the ship's synagogue. The Queen Mary *was the first ship to have a Jewish synagogue included in the original plans.*

Altar of the Second-Class Catholic Chapel. The chapel was in the Second-Class Library, with the altar normally hidden behind a folding wall. The painting behind the altar is entitled Madonna of the Tall Ships.

The largest room ever built on a ship, the Queen Mary's *First-Class Dining Salon is three decks high, 143 feet long, and 118 feet wide. The largest piece of artwork on the ship, seen at the far end of the room, is entitled* Merrie England *by Philip Connard, RA. It depicts, in tapestry style, English country life.*

In a Cunard publicity photo, First-Class passengers enjoy a sumptuous dinner in the Dining Salon.

Celebration of Splendor

The interior treatments of the *Queen Mary*'s passenger accommodations evidenced the radical artistic influences of the 1930s. Yet the new-style decor blended tastefully with the conservative touches that subtly reflected a quiet sophistication.

The ship's interior rooms, decorated with a mix of furnishings, wood paneling, carpeting, and artwork to create a desired setting and mood, were viewed with enthusiastic approval by critics and journalists. "The rooms will be perfectly satisfying to the most cosmopolitan conceptions of culture and good taste, at the same time retaining the atmosphere of restfulness and comfort associated with the most dignified English country homes" (from an untitled booklet, 1935). "Period styles have been discarded in favor of restrained modernism, with a result of subdued elegance" (*The Compass*, 1936).

The major element of the *Queen Mary*'s decor was wood — fifty-six of the world's finest and rarest woods. In every lounge, public room, and passageway, thin wood veneers were used expertly to create a warm and romantic ambience. Wood was so prevalent that the *Queen Mary* was often dubbed "the ship of beautiful woods."

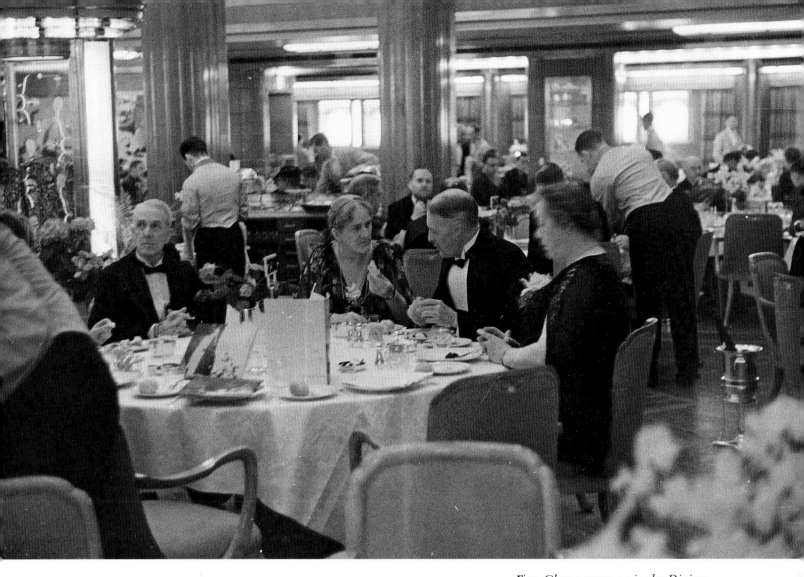

The ship's First-Class main entrance was paneled in masur birch, cross-banded with plain birch, and trimmed in English elm burr dado. Light and dark peroba with maple burr panels lined the First-Class Restaurant. The ship's main staircase was paneled in white English mottled ash, with English elm burr dado and columns. The Promenade Deck's First-Class Shopping Center sported chestnut-oak walls, cross-banded with plain oak, and floor-to ceiling pillars paneled with English elm burr. Mostly popular decorative woods were used in the rooms and hallways, but some rare and little-known woods were also utilized, such as makoré (cherry mahogany), acero, angelim, avodiré, black bean, bubinga, corbaril, ebony, maidu, padouk, synara, thuya, and zebrano.

To complement the lavish wood veneers, Cunard hired a team of more than thirty artists and sculptors to decorate the *Queen Mary*'s passenger compartments. Notable among the group was Doris Zinkeisen, interior designer of the Verandah Grill, who also painted a thirty-foot mural for the room. Her sister, Anna, was commissioned to create four panels for the ballroom, for which she chose the theme "The Four Seasons."

The Main Lounge, one of the most beautiful rooms in the ship, was the social and recreational center for First-Class passengers. During the day, organ recitals or performances by the ship's orchestra filled the lounge with music, and tea was served promptly at 4 P.M. In the evening, the lounge featured bingo or miniature-horse-racing games.

One of the pierced and carved screens by James Woodford for the Smoking Room on the Promenade Deck.

Although the *Queen Mary* had a ballroom, the Main Lounge was also used for dancing. Men in tuxedos and women in formal gowns danced their way romantically across the Atlantic.

Second or Third-Class passengers were allowed in the Main Lounge on Sunday morning when the captain performed a non-denominational church service open to all. The *Queen Mary* was well-equipped to fill the needs of her passengers in all classes. Besides the captain's Sunday service in the Main Lounge, the ship incorporated two Catholic chapels and a Jewish synagogue, and held an Anglican service. Additional space was provided as needed for any religious service required by passengers.

A voyage on the *Queen Mary* was akin to staying in the most luxurious hotel in any of the world's greatest cities. Indeed, the *Queen Mary* was herself a floating city. The size of the great ship caused famed British actress Beatrice Lillie to exclaim, "When does this place get to England?"

From the moment they boarded the *Queen Mary*, passengers were treated like royalty. Bags and trunks were whisked by baggage handlers to passengers' accommodations while bellboys escorted passengers to staterooms or suites. A standard First-Class stateroom on the *Queen Mary* was much larger than the cabins offered on contemporary liners — and larger than modern-day counterparts as well. Each stateroom contained two comfortable single beds, a writing desk, and a small table with overstuffed chairs. Each First-Class stateroom also had a private bathroom containing a tub with shower and a sink. The bathtub had hot and cold running salt water and fresh water, which served two purposes. Firstly, since the ship carried all fresh water in tanks, it helped to conserve water. And, secondly, in the 1930s, salt water was considered to be very therapeutic and many people enjoyed taking a saltwater bath.

The Queen Mary's *gardener oversees a newly arrived batch of plants. The ship's flower shop supplied thousands of potted plants, greenery, and assorted flowers for varied areas of the ship.*

The walls surrounding the tubs were formica, a new and expensive material in 1936 that equates to decorating with marble today. Some towel racks were electrically heated so passengers had hot towels with which to dry themselves after baths. If a passenger needed assistance while in the bathroom, he or she could reach for a small panel near the tub that contained two buttons — red to call a steward and green to summon a stewardess. The ship's wealthy passengers were accustomed to servants helping them with their baths, but many of the *Queen Mary*'s less-worldly passengers were understandably shocked and embarrassed when they accidentally pushed the wrong button.

The Mermaid Bar on the starboard side of the Promenade Deck was a popular rendezvous for Second-Class passengers.

The Suite

The most luxurious and expensive way to travel on the *Queen Mary* was in a First-Class suite. Suites usually consisted of at least four rooms and a luggage closet. Each suite was magnificently furnished and decorated. The master bedroom featured a large marquetry panel, handcrafted of inlaid wood, over the beds. Artists used various hues of the fifty-six types of wood utilized throughout the ship's decor for the panels.

The centerpiece of each suite was the sitting room, a spacious parlor furnished in plush overstuffed sofas and chairs. Decorated with paintings, handmade carpets, and ceramic sculptures, each sitting room was unique and exquisite. The room usually contained an electric fireplace, over which hung a peach-glass mirror. Ostensibly, during inclement weather, when the ship rolled and the passengers were queasy and pale, one glance in the tinted peach-glass mirror at their rosy cheeks would give them a psychological boost.

Included with each suite was at least one maid's room, for passengers who would not consider traveling without personal servants. Of course, these small bedrooms were also perfect for families with children.

Continuing the tradition of unquestioned personal service, Cunard did everything possible to accommodate the tastes of the *Queen Mary*'s First-Class passengers. Favored passengers who requested color and furnishing modifications to their suites were supplied with whatever they wished.

For example, the Duke and Duchess of Windsor always booked suite number M-58 on the Main Deck. The duchess was fond of electric blues and greens, and the suite was decorated especially for her in those colors before each voyage. The *Queen Mary*'s chief steward stored curtains, carpets, and coverlets in dozens of color schemes to satisfy passengers' preferences.

Little did anyone know that soon the *Queen Mary*, with her elegant suites and spacious staterooms, would become the bane of the Nazi hierarchy.

Elegant furnishings pampered First-Class passengers in the Main Lounge.

Opposite page:
A First-Class passenger uses the convenient telephone in her cabin. Through radiotelephone connections, Queen Mary *passengers could call anywhere in the world while at sea. The ship had more than 600 telephones, keeping several operators busy full time.*

Many of the suites had spacious sitting rooms that doubled as private dining rooms.

A First-Class stateroom was large and lavishly decorated with wood paneling and artwork. Each stateroom had its own electric heater, fan, and air louvers.

Stewards at work cleaning the Main Lounge on the Promenade Deck — a major center of activity for First-Class passengers. Towering over the onyx fireplace is a beautiful gesso panel entitled Unicorns in Battle *by Gilbert Bayes and Alfred Oakley.*

A playroom attendant has the toys all lined up and ready for children in the Second-Class Playroom.

Playful *mural painted by George Ramon for*
the First-Class Children's Playroom.

Besides hundreds of toys, dolls, and games, the First-Class Children's Playroom had a projection room where children could watch cartoons.

FAMOUS PASSENGERS

Politicians/Statesmen

Winston Churchill
Anthony Eden, British Foreign Minister
General Dwight D. Eisenhower
Walter S. Gifford, American Ambassador
    in London

Royalty/Socialites

Baron and Baroness Elie de Rothschild
King Faisal II of Iraq
Sir Cedric Hardwicke
Lady Hardwicke
Master E. C. Hardwicke
Duke and Duchess of Windsor

Men and Women of Letters

Noel Coward
Hedda Hopper
W. Somerset Maugham
J.B. Priestly
Earl Wilson

Tycoons and Financiers

Henry Ford, Jr.
Huntington Hartford
Aristotle S. Onassis
Michael Todd
Jack Wrather

Movie Stars

Don Ameche
Annabella
George Arliss
Fred Astaire
Lionel Barrymore
Constance Bennett
Joe E. Brown

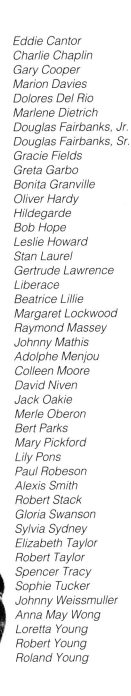

Eddie Cantor
Charlie Chaplin
Gary Cooper
Marion Davies
Dolores Del Rio
Marlene Dietrich
Douglas Fairbanks, Jr.
Douglas Fairbanks, Sr.
Gracie Fields
Greta Garbo
Bonita Granville
Oliver Hardy
Hildegarde
Bob Hope
Leslie Howard
Stan Laurel
Gertrude Lawrence
Liberace
Beatrice Lillie
Margaret Lockwood
Raymond Massey
Johnny Mathis
Adolphe Menjou
Colleen Moore
David Niven
Jack Oakie
Merle Oberon
Bert Parks
Mary Pickford
Lily Pons
Paul Robeson
Alexis Smith
Robert Stack
Gloria Swanson
Sylvia Sydney
Elizabeth Taylor
Robert Taylor
Spencer Tracy
Sophie Tucker
Johnny Weissmuller
Anna May Wong
Loretta Young
Robert Young
Roland Young

Mary Pickford sits at the dressing table in her suite during a crossing in 1937.

Famous actor Lionel Barrymore in the First-Class Main Lounge.

Page 56:
Namesakes of the greatest ocean liners ever built are shown in this photograph taken at Princess Anne's christening. From left to right: Queen Mary, Queen Elizabeth II, and Queen Elizabeth, the Queen Mother.

Previous page:
Famed playwright Noel Coward pauses during an afternoon stroll on the Sports Deck in 1936.

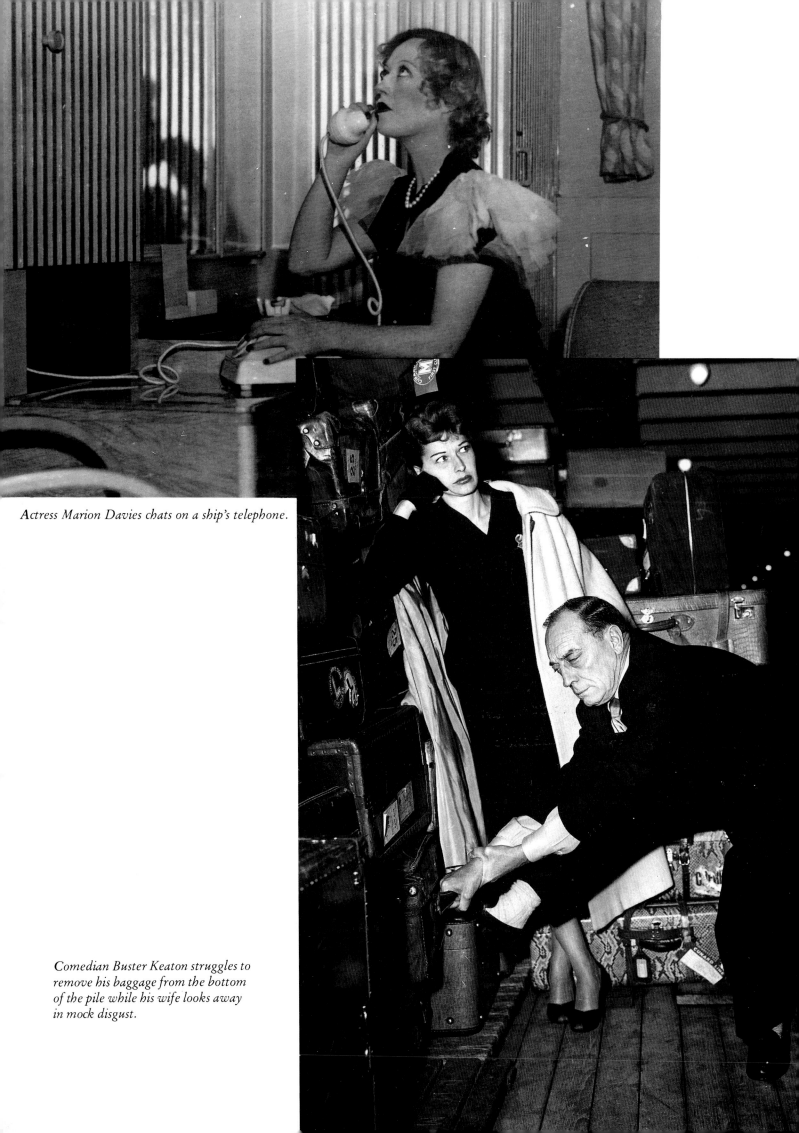

Actress Marion Davies chats on a ship's telephone.

Comedian Buster Keaton struggles to remove his baggage from the bottom of the pile while his wife looks away in mock disgust.

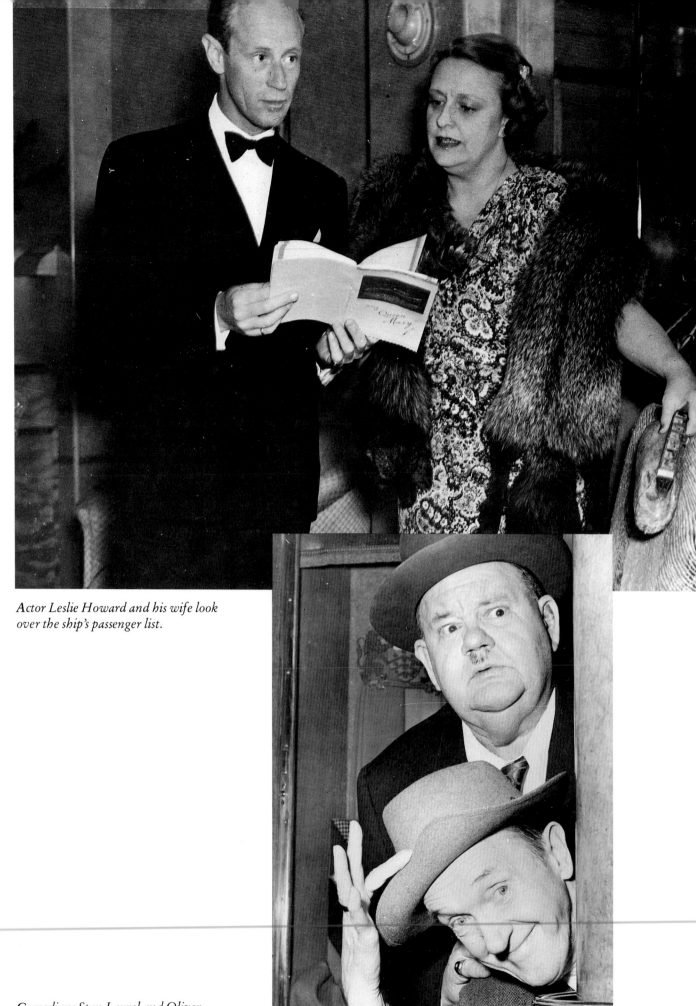

Actor Leslie Howard and his wife look over the ship's passenger list.

Comedians Stan Laurel and Oliver Hardy mug for the ship's photographer.

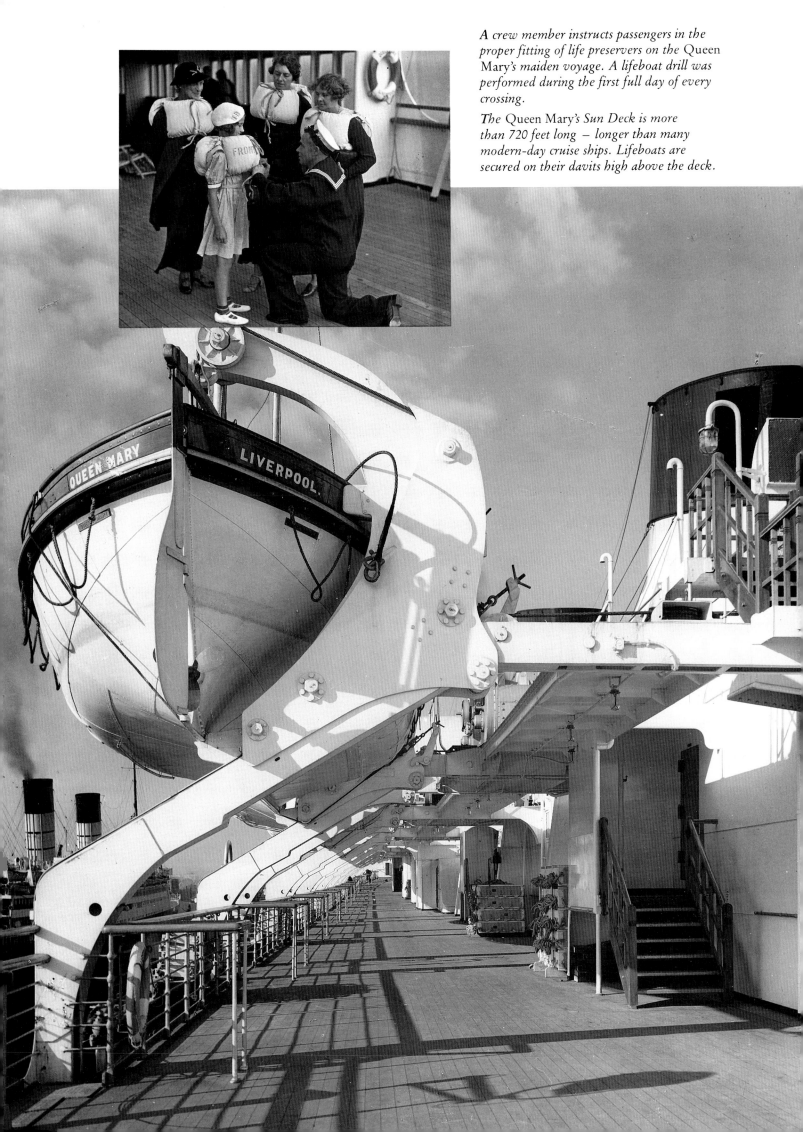

A crew member instructs passengers in the proper fitting of life preservers on the Queen Mary's maiden voyage. A lifeboat drill was performed during the first full day of every crossing.

The Queen Mary's Sun Deck is more than 720 feet long — longer than many modern-day cruise ships. Lifeboats are secured on their davits high above the deck.

Maiden-voyage passengers enjoy a friendly game of quoits on the Sports Deck.

Opposite page:
For passengers wishing to stay in shape during the voyage, the liner had gymnasiums stocked with exercise and athletic equipment. Here, two gentlemen try out the mechanical horses.

As the Queen Mary *sets sail on her maiden voyage on
May 27, 1936, a band plays on the vessel's stern.*

A forward lookout stands near the ship's bell in the fo'c'sle, the most forward part of the ship's bow.

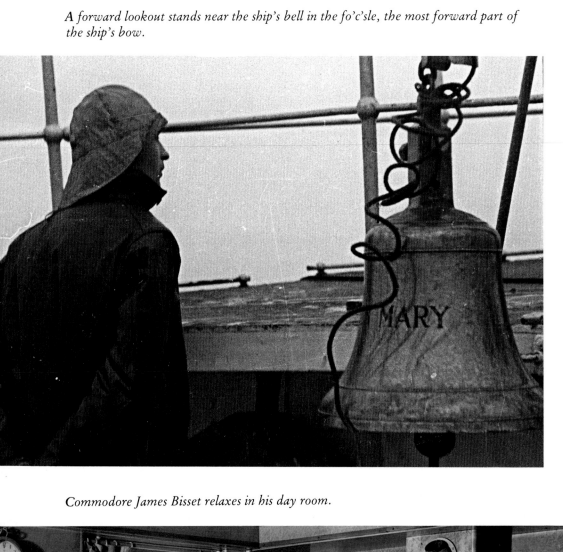

Commodore James Bisset relaxes in his day room.

*Tugboats strain to guide the Queen Mary down river as she heads for the open
sea from the John Brown & Company shipyard on March 24, 1936.*

Faster than most warships, the Queen Mary *usually traveled alone without protection. She relied on secrecy and her great speed to elude enemy ships and planes. The sight of the great liner slipping silently and swiftly across the seas in her camouflage paint earned her the nickname Gray Ghost.*

THE QUEEN MARY

GOES TO WAR

The Second-Class Bar on Main Deck was converted into a dispensary during troopship days.

Chapter III

The summer of 1939 found the *Queen Mary* at the height of her success. All of Cunard's expectations for the giant ship had come true: she was big, she was safe, and she was fast; best of all, she was profitable.

But events in Europe soon cut short the *Queen Mary*'s glamorous career and set her on a new course — a course that would take the *Queen Mary* to seas and ports her builders had never dreamed she would visit — in a role dictated by the grim necessities of war.

For months, the likelihood of war increased as the British government engaged in a hopeless attempt to appease Adolf Hitler's territorial demands. All pretense at negotiation finally ended, however, when Nazi forces launched a surprise invasion of Poland in September 1939.

The *Queen Mary* departed on her last peacetime voyage on August 30, two days before the German attack. As Nazi troops poured into Poland, the *Queen Mary* was in mid-Atlantic bound for New York. The clouds of war had been gathering for some time, and thousands of people were leaving Europe before hostilities broke out. Filled to overflowing, the *Queen Mary* carried a record number of passengers: 2,329. Making the voyage were comedian Bob Hope and his wife. "Dolores and I were in Paris when we were ordered home," he recalls. "We made London in time to catch the *Queen Mary*'s last trip. She was carrying the maximum. Everyone she could crowd. People were actually sleeping in the passageways. I couldn't believe there would be a war, and I said so. Then England declared war."

It was nearly midnight on September 2 when Commodore R. B. Irving received a coded message from the Admiralty ordering him to put the *Queen Mary* on full war alert, and to take every precaution to ensure the liner's safe arrival in New York. The message also warned him to be on the alert for enemy submarines.

Immediately, Commodore Irving ordered the helmsman to steer a zig-zag course and posted additional lookouts to watch for enemy vessels and aircraft. Crewmen were sent to the staterooms and cabins to paint the ship's portholes black. The *Queen Mary*'s running and deck lights were turned off, and the great ship raced in complete darkness for the safety of New York Harbor. The next morning, the passengers listened as the ship's public address system broadcast Prime Minister Neville Chamberlain's fateful message, "This nation is at war with Germany."

With war now official, the *Queen Mary* was a prime target for Nazi submarines. Worried passengers cast fearful glances at the dark sea where, at any moment, a lurking U-boat could launch a deadly attack. The *Queen Mary*'s only defense being her speed, she steamed toward New York at nearly thirty knots. Anxious passengers breathed a sigh of relief when she sailed safely into New York Harbor on September 4, and docked at Pier 90. In the berth next to the *Queen Mary* was her transatlantic rival, the *Normandie*, also taking refuge from the enemy.

Another ship was not as fortunate. Less than ten hours after Chamberlain's proclamation of war, the German submarine *U-30* torpedoed the British liner *Athenia* off the coast of Scotland. One hundred and twelve passengers, including twenty-eight Americans, lost their lives in the first marine casualty of World War II.

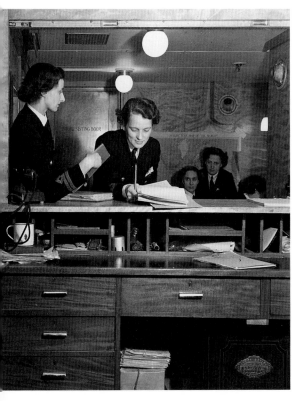

A soldier's original snapshot shows members of the gun crew posing with ammunition for one of the five 40-mm anti-aircraft guns mounted on the Queen Mary.

"Wrens" (Women's Royal Naval Service) working in the Communication Office.

Previous page:
The Queen Mary undergoing wartime conversion in Singapore, 1940. Note the installation of the six-inch gun on the ship's stern.

Most of the Queen Mary's crew soon returned to England and other war-related duties, leaving a small maintenance crew to look after the ship. Since she was a major target for Nazi saboteurs, the ship was placed under twenty-four-hour military guard.

On March 7, 1940, the Queen Mary received a surprise visit from her sister ship, the Queen Elizabeth. The partially finished Queen Elizabeth was in the John Brown & Company shipyard at Clydebank, Scotland, well within range of German bombers from the Continent, when Britain declared war. She left Scotland on March 2, supposedly for sea trials and a short voyage to Southampton. Even her crew was unaware of the true nature of the voyage they were beginning — they were told to pack just enough clothing for the short trip to Southampton.

When the Queen Elizabeth reached the sea, her captain opened sealed orders from the Admiralty commanding him to take the ship immediately and directly to New York, even though the Queen Elizabeth had had no formal sea trials to test her engines, her operating systems, or her crew. Under such conditions, the voyage to America would be hazardous. She secretly crossed the Atlantic without incident however, and upon arriving in New York, the Queen Elizabeth tied up alongside the Queen Mary. They were a spectacular sight, both now painted in wartime gray; the Normandie, in striking contrast, still wore her peacetime colors.

In Britain, great controversy raged about the use of the giant passenger liners. Many Admiralty and government authorities felt the vessels were too valuable to be used as troopships. Some even suggested that they be sold to raise money for the war effort. But all soon realized that the sister ships were much too valuable as transports to be wasted.

The situation in England had become critical. The British army was nearly destroyed at Dunkirk, and Hitler's powerful army was poised on the Continent, ready to advance on Britain at the Führer's command.

The Queen Mary was quickly drafted into war service, her size and usefulness as a troop transport outweighing the danger. On March 21, 1940, the Queen Mary silently slipped down the Hudson to the open sea and turned south. Her departure and destination were top secret.

As she sped away from New York, the Queen Mary was undergoing unusual alterations. She had already been camouflaged with a coat of gray paint, and her two-and-a-half-foot-high name obliterated. Soon she would be known by the apt nom de guerre of the Gray Ghost, scourge of the Nazi U-boats. Racing across the sea or slipping silently in and out of the fog, no sooner was her profile sighted by enemy vessels than she seemed to magically disappear.

The fastest ship afloat, the Queen Mary could race at more than thirty knots (34.5 MPH/55.6 kmph) and maintain that incredible speed for thousands of miles. In the early days of the war, she was actually faster than German torpedoes.

After a refueling stop in Cape Town, South Africa, the *Queen Mary* sailed for Sydney, Australia, where her luxurious fittings were removed and she was converted into a troopship capable of transporting 5,000 soldiers.

Special sound-detection sonar was installed to allow the ship to pinpoint submerged enemy submarines so she could maneuver to avoid them. Unfortunately, the sonar proved ineffective; the *Queen Mary*'s massive propellers were too noisy for the sonar system to operate properly.

Anti-aircraft machine guns were mounted in strategic locations on the upper decks, and a small six-inch gun was anchored to the *Queen Mary*'s stern. Although useless against a concerted attack by submarine, aircraft, or warship, the six-inch armament would be handy against a small vessel or reconnaissance aircraft. To protect her from magnetic mines, an electronic degaussing, or demagnetizing, strip was attached to the ship's hull to repel underwater explosives.

When the conversion was complete, 5,000 Australian troops boarded and the *Queen Mary* began her first voyage as a troop carrier.

Faced with the possibility of invasion, Great Britain needed every soldier available in her far-reaching commonwealth. Thus, on the morning of May 4, 1940, the *Queen Mary* sailed with the liners *Aquitania, Mauretania, Empress of Japan, Empress of Canada*, and *Empress of Britain* — also recently converted to troopships — escorted by a group of warships. The liners called at Fremantle, Australia, for supplies and additional troops, then sailed for Scotland with refueling stops at Cape Town, Simonstown, and Freetown.

On the same day the *Queen Mary* dropped anchor in Gourock, Scotland, war-torn France appealed to Hitler for an armistice. Allied troops evacuated Norway, Italy declared war on England, and Britain was desperately short of manpower and material.

Following a stay of thirteen days in Gourock, the *Queen Mary* was ordered to Singapore to dry-dock for a much-needed cleaning. Sailing from Scotland on June 29, 1940, she completed the 14,000-mile voyage without mishap and was placed in Singapore's giant dry dock on August 5. The next forty-one days were filled with frantic activity as workmen cleaned the ship's hull, and mechanics and engineers overhauled her engines, boilers, and steering mechanisms. Later, in Sydney, a set of para-

The three largest passenger liners ever built, at berth in New York in March, 1940. Left to right are the Normandie, *the* Queen Mary, *and the* Queen Elizabeth.

vanes was attached to the *Queen Mary's* bow to augment the degaussing strips. Consisting of two floating devices shaped like torpedoes, the paravanes were towed from the ship's bow. As the ship moved through the water, they spread out on either side of the vessel. The paravanes' towing cables intercepted any mines along the ship's course and cut their anchor lines, causing the mines to bob to the surface where they could be destroyed by gunfire from the *Queen Mary's* decks.

When the Italian army invaded Egypt on September 14, 1940, British military leaders were shocked. Suddenly, the entire direction of the war changed. With the Italians in North Africa, the vital Suez Canal was in danger of being captured by the Axis powers.

After the Italian invasion of Africa, the *Queen Elizabeth*, still docked in New York Harbor, was prepared for war service. She sailed for Singapore for conversion and continued to Sydney for final fitting out as a troopship.

The *Queen Mary* met her bigger sister at sea for the first time in April 1941 off the Australian coast at Sydney Head. The two giant sisterships sailed together on April 9, 1941, carrying a combined troop complement of 10,000 New Zealand and Australian soldiers. On this voyage, the ships were in convoy with the Cunarder *Mauretania*. For the remainder of 1941, the *Queen Mary* made Sydney her home port and continued to ferry troops and supplies to the Middle East.

Although the danger to the *Queen Mary* from enemy aircraft or submarines was great, temperature was an even greater threat on the Sydney-to-Suez voyages. Designed to ply the cold North Atlantic, the *Queen Mary* had not been equipped with adequate air conditioning for the hot climate through which she was now sailing. Allied troops and German prisoners suffered horribly from the suffocating heat below decks. Harry Grattidge, the *Queen Mary's* staff captain on many of these voyages, often assisted the ship's sole chaplain in the solemn task of burying the dead at sea. In his book, *Captain of the Queens*, he writes, "Almost every four hours came news of another death. Both the bosun and the deck storekeeper, who prepare bodies for a burial, were almost rushed off their feet... four times a day I was forced to intone the gravest words that a ship's officer can utter, "Man that is born of woman has but a short time to live'."

Japan's surprise attack on Pearl Harbor on December 7, 1941, and the destruction of the U.S. Pacific fleet forced drastic changes in British war strategy. Thus far, British shipping vessels had sailed the Pacific and southern seas in virtual safety, the only danger being a chance encounter with a long-range German warship or submarine. Japan's entry into the

Thousands of soldiers crowd the bow of the ship during a lifeboat drill. Although the Queen Mary *carried extra lifeboats and dozens of inflatable rafts, her sinking could have resulted in thousands of fatalities.*

war on the side of the Axis coalition changed that. The British Pacific colonies, including Singapore, were immediately endangered. Even Australia, weakened by the great number of troops sent to other war fronts, was in danger of invasion by Japanese forces.

Soon after the attack on Pearl Harbor, the *Queen Mary* was turned over to American military commanders. She remained under the command of her British captain and crew, but her duties and destinations were determined by American authorities.

The *Queen Mary* was moved to the Boston Navy Yard for an extensive refitting. Her troop capacity was increased to 8,200, with metal standee berths being erected in drawing rooms, in lounges, and even in drained swimming pools.

May 1942. Photo shows some defensive armament along the port side of the Queen Mary.

As the Queen Mary *approached dangerous coastlines, British or American aircraft met the ship to offer air support and protection from enemy submarines.*

Gun crews rush to stations "on the double" during an exercise. Guns were manned by both British and American gunners.

View of the Queen Mary *at full speed, taken from the bridge of the British cruiser HMS* Scylla *in May 1943. On board the* Queen Mary *were Prime Minister Winston Churchill and his party, en route to New York and Washington to meet with President Roosevelt.*

The *Queen Mary*'s armament was also improved. Five 40mm double-barreled cannons were installed; two on the bow, two on the stern, and one above the bridge. Twenty-four 20mm guns were mounted in strategic positions on the ship's upper decks. Six three-inch guns augmented the six-inch cannon and the many .50 and .30-caliber machine guns already aboard. Near the after funnel (smokestack), four sets of anti-aircraft rocket launchers were installed. Many years later, a member of the gun crew recalled, "The pillar boxes had twin cradles for twenty rockets each, which were fired electrically and were adapted for high-angle and low-angle targets."

Refitted and newly armed, the *Queen Mary* embarked 8,398 soldiers and sailed northeast out of Boston on February 18, 1942. As soon as she sailed out of sight of land, the *Queen Mary* turned sharply south, proceeding to Trinidad. Her destination was Sydney, where her passengers and cargo (artillerymen and ordnance supplies) were sorely needed.

As the *Queen Mary* neared Trinidad, heavy U-boat activity was reported and she was rerouted to Key West. While in Florida, the ship took on fuel, provisions, and a new captain. The ship's captain, John Townley, having reached mandatory retirement age, was replaced by James Bisset.

Leaving Key West, Captain Bisset steered the *Queen Mary* on a winding course through the Caribbean, finally traversing the narrow Anegada Passage to the open sea. Less than a half-hour later, the *Queen Mary*'s radioman intercepted a distress signal from a torpedoed steamer ten miles astern of the liner's course. The enemy was near.

The presence of the Axis powers was also felt in Rio de Janeiro. While the *Queen Mary* refueled and replenished her stores, Axis spies plotted to destroy her. Using a radio hidden in the hills above the port, they signalled the *Queen Mary*'s course and departure time to their comrades just minutes before being captured by Allied authorities. Captain Bisset, warned that the ship's departure time had been revealed to the enemy, finished refueling, then sailed several hours early.

The *Queen Mary* got safely away, but a tanker leaving Rio at her scheduled departure time was torpedoed by a German submarine waiting outside the harbor. So certain were the Axis authorities of the *Queen Mary*'s destruction that one Japanese radio station actually reported she had been sunk. On board the *Queen Mary*, safely at sea, a radioman rushed onto the bridge and exclaimed, "Sir, I've just received a radio message that we have been torpedoed and sunk." Captain Bisset calmly replied, "Keep it under your hat. Don't let the troops know that we've been sunk. It might worry them."

Always vulnerable to torpedo attacks, the *Queen Mary* kept moving at all times. During one return crossing to New York in May 1942, five lifeboats from a torpedoed steamer were sighted. Knowing that a submarine could be waiting nearby, Captain Bisset did not stop to rescue the survivors, but signaled to them that he would radio their position to rescue vessels. One of the survivors was the son of the *Queen Mary*'s chief purser, who, after being rescued by an American naval vessel, sent a message to his father aboard the *Queen Mary*: "Dad useless as usual. Passed us by. But we made it."

Dramatic photograph of the burning forward section of the light cruiser HMS Curacoa *after being struck by the* Queen Mary.

In late 1942 the *Queen Mary* was once again traveling her accustomed route on the North Atlantic. A massive troop buildup had begun, and the ship was needed to transport American and Canadian soldiers to England. To expedite the buildup, American and British military leaders considered increasing both the *Queen Mary* and the *Queen Elizabeth*'s troop capacity to 10,000 each. American General George C. Marshall, worried about the risk of losing so many men if either ship was torpedoed, consulted with Prime Minister Winston Churchill, who told him that if it could shorten the war by even one day, the risk was worth taking. Marshall decided to pay a personal visit to the *Queen Mary* and see for himself the potential problems of carrying 10,000 troops.

The biggest problem of transporting so many men, explained Staff Captain Harry Grattidge, was crossing the Holland Tunnel beneath the Hudson River. So fully loaded, the ship's keel would be very near the top of the tunnel. If the men lined the ship's side as they normally did, the ship would list, increasing her draft, and she would most likely strike the tunnel. General Marshall solved the problem in a unique manner. As the ship neared the tunnel, the vessel's army commander shouted into the public address system, "All troops, attention!" While the *Queen Mary* sailed safely over the tunnel, her military personnel stood perfectly still.

On all transatlantic voyages, the *Queen Mary* traveled alone, without escort. For most warships to accompany the swift liner, she would have had to travel at reduced speed, a real danger in submarine-infested waters. So, the *Queen Mary* would leave New York with protective destroyers and aircraft following her as far as they could. When she arrived off the coast of Scotland, she would again be met by protective aircraft and warships as she approached the coastline.

Miraculously, the *Queen Mary* encountered only one serious accident during the war, in October 1942. Approaching the coast of Scotland, with 10,000 American troops aboard, she was met by a small flotilla of destroyers equipped to defend the liner from submarine attack, if necessary. Leading the flotilla was the 4,290-ton British anti-aircraft cruiser HMS *Curacoa*. Procedure called for the destroyers to form a protective cordon around the *Queen Mary*, and the *Curacoa*, armed with heavy anti-aircraft guns, remained near in case enemy aircraft were spotted.

Suddenly, before anyone on either ship realized the danger, the *Queen Mary*, still on a zig-zag course, and the *Curacoa* converged at high speed. The force of the giant liner's striking the 450-foot-long warship 150 feet forward of the cruiser's stern spun the *Curacoa* broadside to the *Queen Mary*'s massive bow. Like a hot knife slicing through butter, the *Queen Mary* cut the *Curacoa* in half, plowing straight through stricken cruiser.

Many of the *Curacoa*'s crew died instantly, trapped below decks by the onslaught of cold seawater. Two crewmen, unable to escape through the ship's regular passages, crawled into a hatch leading into one of the vessel's funnels. Making their way through the narrow passage and out onto the

Opposite page:
The crushed bow of the Queen Mary *after the collision with the cruiser HMS* Curacoa. *The photograph was taken during repairs in the dry dock at Boston Harbor.*

side of the foundering ship, they slid down the ship's hull into the water along with dozens of their comrades.

On the upper decks of the *Queen Mary*, horrified soldiers and crewmen watched as the two halves of the *Curacoa* bobbed astern, sinking rapidly. Some quick-thinking soldiers hurled life preservers into the sea, hoping to aid the men in the water. The two halves of the *Curacoa* sunk in less than five minutes.

On the bridge of the *Queen Mary*, Captain Cyril Illingworth was faced with a difficult decision. Should he stop and lower lifeboats to save the seamen struggling in the water? On board the *Queen Mary* were 10,000 soldiers whose safety depended on him, and they were sailing in a favorite sea lair of Nazi U-boats. Captain Illingworth made the only decision he could. The *Queen Mary* sailed on, but sent a radio message to the other vessels to rescue the *Curacoa* survivors.

Captain Illingworth was faced with another serious question. How badly damaged was the *Queen Mary*? He knew she could not have cut through an armor-plated cruiser without sustaining serious damage to her bow. Illingworth sent Staff Captain Grattidge forward to inspect the damage, and, as a safety precaution, reduced the liner's speed.

When Grattidge arrived on the scene, he was relieved. The ship had a gaping hole in her bow, but the shattered steel plates had folded back into

Although gambling was strictly forbidden aboard, American soldiers take time out for their favorite pastime while relaxing on standee berths. With as little as eighteen inches of clearance between berths, it was possible to bunk twenty-one soldiers in a First-Class cabin intended for two passengers.

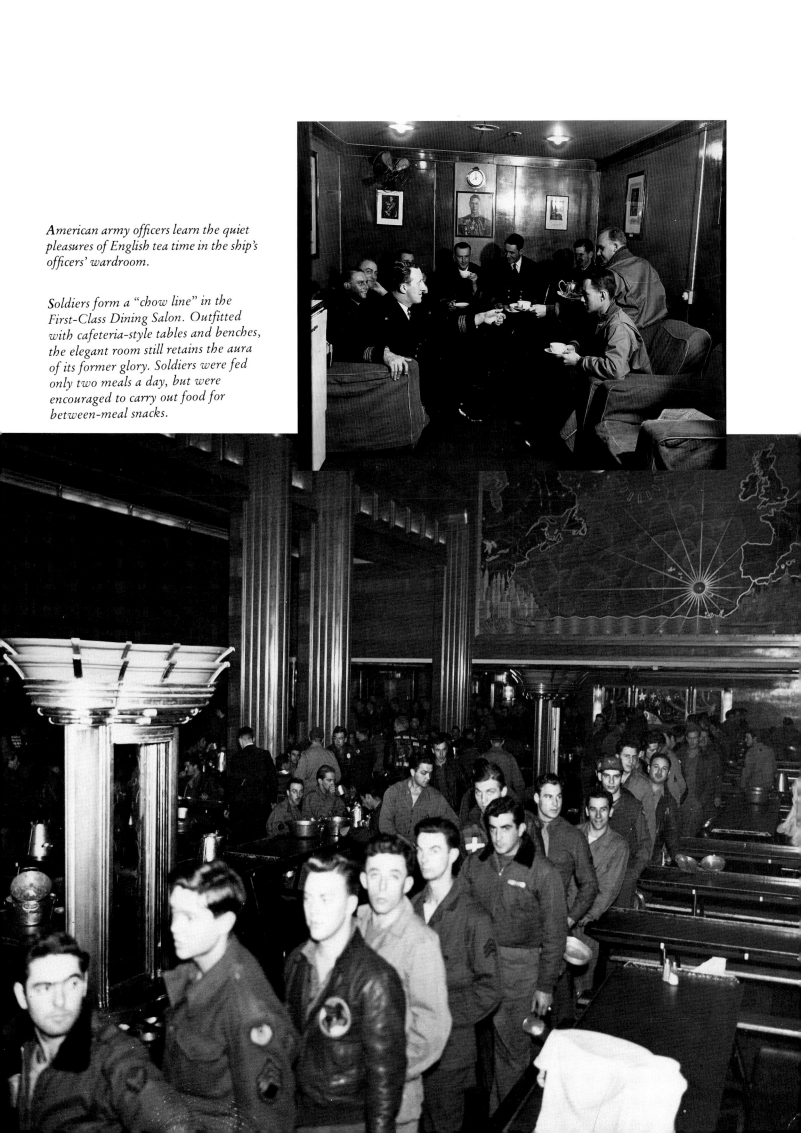

American army officers learn the quiet pleasures of English tea time in the ship's officers' wardroom.

Soldiers form a "chow line" in the First-Class Dining Salon. Outfitted with cafeteria-style tables and benches, the elegant room still retains the aura of its former glory. Soldiers were fed only two meals a day, but were encouraged to carry out food for between-meal snacks.

the hole, partially closing it. Water surged in and out of the hole, but the ship's forward collision bulkhead was holding. If the bulkhead had been smashed by the crash or the pounding of the incoming waves, the ship might not have survived. Grattidge immediately ordered reinforcement of the bulkhead, and the *Queen Mary* continued on to Gourock, Scotland, at half speed. With no facilities available to repair the damaged bow plates, workmen had to make temporary repairs. Tons of cement were poured into the hole to seal it. The *Queen Mary* then sailed to the Boston Naval Yard at twenty-one knots (24.2 MPH/38.9 kmph) for permanent repairs.

Even though the nearby destroyers moved in quickly to rescue the *Curacoa*'s crew, loss of life was great. Of the more than 400 officers and men aboard, 338 died. The official investigation produced contradictory findings. At first, responsibility for the collision was determined to lay with the captain of the *Curacoa*, reasoning the warship should have stayed clear of the *Queen Mary*. Later, the final settlement apportioned two-thirds of the responsibility to the *Curacoa* and one-third to the *Queen Mary*. It was a decision that cost Cunard thousands of pounds in compensation for damages.

The collision was one of the war's best-kept secrets. Fearful that the Axis powers would use the incident for propaganda purposes, the Allies clamped a tight security lid on all details of the accident until after the war.

The Allied need for more soldiers and supplies in Great Britain was insatiable. To fulfill this demand, the *Queen Mary*'s troop-carrying capabilities were once again increased — to 15,000. For the first time in history, an entire division was transported on a single ship. The *Queen Mary* set a record on July 25, 1943, sailing from New York to Gourock with 15,740 passengers and a crew of 943 aboard, a total of 16,683 persons. The record stands today as the greatest number of people ever embarked on a ship for any voyage.

The *Queen Mary* and her sister ship, the *Queen Elizabeth*, were both plying the transatlantic route carrying 15,000 each in summer and 10,000 in winter. The *Queen Mary*'s schedule was almost as regular as it had been before the war. She would arrive in New York Harbor in the afternoon, embark troops, refuel and load supplies, then sail with the morning tide — all in less than ninety-six hours, with the 15,000 troops embarking in less than twelve hours. Upon awakening, sleepy-eyed New Yorkers would gaze at the *Queen Mary*'s empty berth and wonder if they had merely dreamed her the night before.

It was little wonder that the *Queen Mary* was known as the Gray Ghost. She sailed into New York Harbor unannounced and departed without warning, slipping silently away in the early morning mist.

During her numerous New York-to-Gourock voyages, the *Queen Mary* served double duty. On the westbound crossing, she carried thousands of German prisoners of war to detention centers in the United States. Wounded soldiers cared for by the ship's expert hospital staff were also sent home on the *Queen Mary*.

The former Second-Class Children's Playroom takes on a new role as the Royal Air Force's orderly room.

Loaded down with as many as she can carry, the Queen Mary sets out on another wartime voyage across the Atlantic. The liner would often carry more than 15,000 troops on a single crossing, and still holds the record for the most people ever carried on a ship (16,683).

Gin Rummy Aboard Ship *by Robert Bizinsky. This pen-and-ink drawing is one of many created by the famous post-impressionist artist during a 1942 Queen Mary voyage. As an American soldier, Bizinsky served in England, North Africa, and the Middle East. His wartime drawings are a sensitive look at the personal side of men at war.*

OCEAN DAILY NEWS

EDITOR: 1ST. LIEUT. RALPH BLANCHARD

OFFICE: STUDIO, PROMENADE DECK

THURSDAY, MARCH 19, 1942

ASST. EDITOR: PVT. JAMES C. KURZ

NO. 21.

GENERAL MacARTHUR NOW IN AUSTRALIA TO COMMAND LAND, SEA, AIR FORCES OF ALLIES AT REQUEST OF AUSTRALIAN GOVERNMENT

REDS TIGHTEN HOLD ON 16th GERMAN ARMY

The Russians are drawing the ring of steel tighter around the 16th German Army, trapped in the Staraya Russa sector. Thousands of Germans have been wiped out, and 80 places have been liberated in two weeks.

All attempts by the Germans to send reinforcements have failed. In the last fortnight, 90 German planes, most of them Junkers transports, have been shot down. Moscow reports a terrific battle for a city in the south west. In an attack, the Russians have taken an important junction. The Russians have laid down an extremely heavy barrage in the Donets Sector.

Many Germans have been killed on the Kalinin front. German newspaper accounts have strengthened the Russian reports. Switzerland reports that a new cold front exists in Russia. Tanks are frozen solid in the ground. It is 13 degrees below zero in the Crimea.

★ ★ ★

Previous Condition of Servitude!

Lieut. Col. C. H. Cowart, C.O. of the 104th CA Battalion (Sep.), was the branch sales manager for Remington Rand, Inc., at Birmingham, Ala. His territory included Mobile, Ala., Meridan, Miss., and Pensecola, Fla.

Lieut. R. E. Cloud, S-2 of the 104th CA Battalion (Sep.), played no favorites in choosing his work. His selection included selling coke, surveying, junior chemist, bank teller, assistant cashier of the City of Birmingham, Ala., and salesman for the Penn Mutual Life Insurance Co.

Lieut. C. P. Cleveland, Jr., Aide-de-Camp to General Van Volkenburgh, bears a financial background. He graduated in the class of '35 from the Citadel and served as book-keeper for the Citizens & Southern National Bank of South Carolina at Spartanburg, S.C. He later entered the General Financial & Trust in the same city.

1st Lieut. Grady Wright, the ever busy director of the muscle department, toiled for the Fire Insurance Underwriters at Atlanta, Ga.

★ ★ ★

CHESS TOURNAMENT

All men who entered the Chess tournament will report at Prom. Deck, starboard side, aft of the ... Lounge, at 7.30 tonight.

Draw Capsules From Fishbowl

The drawing of 7,000 capsules from the giant fish bowl took place last night in the third draft of this war. This draft will accomodate those men who registered on February 16. The honor of drawing the first capsule falls to Secretary of war Henry L. Stimson, and Director of selective service, Hershey, will make the speech of the evening. 17½ million men were registered in the first two calls.

Daily Lenten Bible Reading

"The Lord is good, a stronghold in the day of trouble; and he knoweth them that trust in him." Nah. 1:7.

AMERICANS RUSH TO PAY INCOME TAX

Americans are rushing to get their income taxes fully paid early in order that the money can go into the war effort. $1,700,000 was collected in income tax in the first two weeks of this month. This more than doubles the sum paid in the same period last year.

In one town in Indiana some 155,000 blanks have been filled in as against 51,300 by this time of last year. $2,700,000,000 in income tax is expected this year.

Speaking of money, President Roosevelt is asking Congress for $17,500,000 for armaments. It is expected that 60,000 planes will be built in 1942 and 120,000 in 1943.

Major-General Wainwright Commands Philippines

General Douglas MacArthur has arrived in Australia and will command the Allied Nations' land, sea and air forces in the Anzac area and the Philippines at the request of the Australian Government, according to an announcement made by the War Department in Washington. In his new position General MacArthur will have powers similar to those of General Wavell in India.

Accompanying General MacArthur on his arrival in Australia were Mrs. MacArthur, their son, Major-General Richard Sutherland, Chief of Staff, and Brigadier-General H. H. George of the Air Corps.

Major-General Wainwright was named to succeed General MacArthur in command of the Bataan forces. The announcement made it clear that this in no way means that the Bataan Peninsula is lost. General Wainwright is one of the best students of modern war technique.

This new appointment is a tribute to General MacArthur's heroic resistance which has fired the imagination of the whole free world. With a small land force and a few planes he was able to accomplish stupendous deeds. He has wiped out whole regiments of Japanese troops.

General MacArthur was given command of the US Army in the Far East last July. He is 62 years old and was the youngest Chief of Staff the United States ever had up to the time of his retirement in 1937. The General has received 13 decorations for bravery under fire and several citations for leading the "Rainbow" Division in F...

Dutch troops have ... Australia from the East ... take their place in the ... Australian, British ar... troops already there...

In the raid on ... day the Japs dro... ation bombs. T... is designed to ex... causing maxim... the raid two ... and eleven w... Jap force... on the Ph... Jap artill... the Peni...

DALTON ANNOUNCES POWER RATIONING

Sir Hugh Dalton, who is in charge of rationing in England, has announced that power consumption in England must be cut. Coal, gas and electricity will all be under the strictest rationing regulations. Dalton says, "Without coal, there can be no arms." 50% of the power consumption is now going into arms production and the people are accepting new rationing gladly.

Clothing, too, will receive a 25% cut. It is believed that this cut in the clothing rations will permit greater space in the ships for arms material.

Indications are that a shortage of wheat may soon exist in England.

AUSTRALIAN MONEY VALUE

For the information of the members of this command, a description of the currency and coins, in more or less common circulation in Australia, is stated below:—

Description	Written Reference	Slang Reference		US Value
Five Pound Note	£5/0/0	Fiver		$16.00
One Pound Note	£1/0/0	Quid		$3.20
Half Pound Note or Ten Shilling Note	£0/10/0 or 10/-	Ten Bob		$1.60
Crown (silver coin)	£0/5/0 or 5/-	Five Bob		$0.80
Two Shilling coin (silver) or Florin	£0/2/0 or 2/-	Two Bob		$0.32
One Shilling coin (silver)	£0/1/0 or 1/-	Bob		$0.16
Six Penny coin (silver)	£0/0/6 or 6d			$0.08
Three Penny coin (silver)	£0/0/3 or 3d		Copper	$0.04
One Penny coin (copper)	£0/0/1 or 1d			$0.013
Half Penny coin (copper)	£0/0/0½ or ½d			$0.0065

In comparing Australian coins with American coins in size, it is noted that the crown is the same size as our silver dollar, the florin is similar in size to our half dollar, and the shilling compares with our quarter, the six pence coin is of the same size as our dime, the three pence coin being smaller, the two copper coins, the penny and half penny, are unusually large for their relative value, the penny is as large as our half dollar and the half penny is the size of our quarter. Arrangements will be made for the conversion of American money into Australian by members of this command.

The ship's printing presses were used to keep the soldiers aboard informed about both world events and everyday events on the Queen Mary. The Ocean Daily News was printed by an American staff, and each issue was eagerly awaited by news-hungry troops.

84

Map shows ports of call visited during the Queen Mary's wartime voyages.

OCEAN DAILY NEWS

EDITORIAL OFFICE : PICCADILLY CIRCUS, PROMENADE DECK

No. 8

MONDAY, JANUARY 4, 1943

ONE PENNY

Hitler Threatens His Retreating Troops

WARNS OF REPRISALS AGAINST FAMILIES

LONDON, SUNDAY.

Driven to desperate measures by the continued advances of the Red Army, Hitler has now threatened to have shot by their own comrades any of his troops who retreat or try to surrender, and has added a warning that reprisals will also be taken against their families.

These threats were made by the German Commander on the Central Russian front during the battle for Velikie Luki, the most important German base in this sector.

Battered by the Russian troops and threatened by their own leaders, the Nazis fought furiously but unavailingly. The town fell to the Red A.... fiercest batt... war, and th... supply colum... their way t... streets.

Latest M... state that th... vancing west... are within 15... the Leningrad... railway.

If this offens... cessfully, the... cation link be... and the Cent... seriously threat...

Further repo... position of the... in the Rzhev sa... the Don and V... more serious.

In the Lower... Red Army is w... Simienskya. It... that the German... early last summe... attack on Stalin... sector the Russi... the capture of... Volga—Black S... miles from Kotel... After bitter... Caucasus, Sovie... ...cupied a di..... have made rapid... area of the Kalmu... tween the Caspian... Caucasus.

BRITISH RAID BEHIND ENEMY LINES

The story has now been published of how, in the early days of the battle of El Alamein last November, two squadrons of light British...

NAZI DIPLOMATS SACKED

The German ambassadors to Japan, Spain and Sweden, have been replaced. These changes do not seem to be due to personal reasons, but appear to reflect Hitler's anger at the state of German relations with these countries.

Japan has failed to co-ordinate with Germany and Italy, and has refused to take part in the war against Russia.

Spain has refused to take any action which might bring her into conflict with the Allied nations.

Sweden has refused any further credits to Germany until June next and made deliveries to Germany dependent on G...

Belgian Judges' Strike Succeeds

The strike of over a thousand Belgian judges and magistrates, reported in the *Ocean Daily News*, has been successful.

The strike arose because the Belgian Supreme Court declared certain German decrees illegal. The members of the Court were imprisoned, and all their fellow judges struck work in sympathy. The judicial system came to a complete standstill, and the Germans had to rescind several of the decrees made.

This is the third success...

NEWS IN...

In New Guinea... have now broken... Japanese resistance... The first French co... a British port since... France has now arri... Bathurst. It had... Dakar, which is n... the Allies.

R. A. F. fighters... sweeps over Northe... yesterday, without los... umber of enemy planes were... ighted, but these did not attempt... ny opposition.

WARTIME VOYAGES.

NEW YORK, TRINIDAD, CAPETOWN, FREMANTLE, SYDNEY.

SYDNEY, FREMANTLE, CAPETOWN, SIMONSTOWN, FREETOWN, CLYDE.

CLYDE, FREETOWN, CAPETOWN, SIMONSTOWN, TRINCOMALEE, SINGAPORE, SYDNEY.

SYDNEY, FREMANTLE, BOMBAY, FREMANTLE, SYDNEY.

SYDNEY, FREMANTLE, TRINCOMALEE, FREMANTLE, SYDNEY.

SYDNEY, SINGAPORE, FREMANTLE, SYDNEY.

SYDNEY, FREMANTLE, TRINCOMALEE, SUEZ, TRINCOMALEE, FREMANTLE, SYDNEY.

SYDNEY, HOBART, SYDNEY, FREMANTLE, TRINCOMALEE, SUEZ, TRINCOMALEE, FREMANTLE, SYDNEY, (2 voyages).

SYDNEY, HOBART, SYDNEY, FREMANTLE, TRINCOMALEE, SUEZ, TRINCOMALEE.

TRINCOMALEE, CAPETOWN, TRINIDAD, NEW YORK.

NEW YORK, BOSTON, KEY WEST, RIO DE JANEIRO, CAPETOWN, FREMANTLE, SYDNEY.

SYDNEY, FREMANTLE, CAPETOWN, RIO DE JANEIRO, NEW YORK.

NEW YORK, CLYDE.

CLYDE, FREETOWN, SIMONSTOWN, SUEZ, SIMONSTOWN, RIO DE JANEIRO, NEW YORK.

NEW YORK, CLYDE.

CLYDE, NEW YORK, CLYDE, (2 voyages).

CLYDE, BOSTON, NEW YORK, CLYDE.

CLYDE, FREETOWN, CAPETOWN, ADEN, SUEZ, MASSAWA, H.M. BASE EAST INDIES, FREMANTLE, SYDNEY, FREMANTLE, CAPETOWN, FREETOWN, CLYDE.

CLYDE, NEW YORK OR HALIFAX, CLYDE, (28 voyages).

... imagination.

Believe only what you read in the *Ocean Daily News*, and remember—Rumour Lies!

... up-top " and " down-below."

You would be wrong if you spoke of the "sharp" or the "blunt" end. They are known as the bows or the stern.

... has just begun, we are "weighing the anchor." As soon as it is clear of the water, but not secured, then it is "aweigh." Not until it is secured for sea is it said to be "weighed."

Loaded with 10,000 to 15,000 passengers, the conditions aboard the *Queen Mary* were extremely crowded. To accommodate the extraordinary number of men, each standee berth had two or three occupants, sleeping in shifts. The berths were stacked up to six high with only eighteen inches of space between them. To turn over in the middle of the night, one had to get out of bed. Yet, with 15,000 aboard, enough berths were not available, even with the men sleeping in shifts. Thousands of soldiers had to bed down on the ship's upper decks. A rotation system was implemented whereby a man would sleep one night on deck and the next night in a berth. Many men preferred sleeping on the upper decks because they felt they would be safer if the *Queen Mary* was torpedoed.

The system devised by the British crew and American military commanders of the *Queen Mary* to achieve the highest efficiency and comfort on the overcrowded ship was ingenious. The *Queen Mary* was divided into red, white, and blue zones, with each man issued a button in one of three colors. He was restricted to that zone of the ship. The system made it possible to load the *Queen Mary* in New York and unload in Gourock in amazingly short periods of time.

The troops were served two meals a day — breakfast and dinner. At each meal, the men took extra servings of fruit and snacks to eat during the long period between meals. Still, the amount of food needed for each voyage was staggering. During the five-day crossing, the men consumed 155,000 pounds of meat and poultry; 21,500 pounds of bacon and ham; 124,000 pounds of potatoes; 76,000 pounds of flour and cereals; 53,000 pounds of butter, eggs, and powdered milk; 31,000 pounds of coffee, tea, and sugar; 31,000 pounds of canned fruit; 18,000 pounds of jams and jellies; 4,600 pounds of cheese; 400 pounds of candy; 5,000 cartons of cigarettes; and 40,000 bottles of soft drinks.

Meal preparation for passengers and crew put a dreadful strain on the ship's catering department. Cooks worked around the clock in shifts — as breakfast was being served, a host of cooks and assistants were preparing the next meal.

During her wartime service, the *Queen Mary* hosted Prime Minister Winston Churchill three times when he crossed to the United States and Canada to attend war conferences. Churchill always traveled under the pseudonym Colonel Warden, a code name used to confuse enemy agents interested in the *Queen Mary*'s passenger list. In May 1943, August 1943, and September 1944, Churchill sailed aboard the *Queen Mary* to the Trident, Quadrant, and Octagon war conferences for top-secret meetings with upper-level American and other Allied war leaders. While aboard the *Queen Mary* in August 1943, Churchill first reviewed the plans for the D-Day invasion and affixed his signature.

Opposite page:
Escort ships and an anti-submarine blimp greet
the Queen Mary *as she nears New York Harbor.*

So effective was she as a troopship, Adolf Hitler put a bounty on the *Queen Mary*. He promised Germany's highest military honor, the Knight's Cross to the Iron Cross with Oak Leaves and Swords, to anyone who could sink her. As an added incentive, he also offered a cash reward of $250,000. But the liner used her great speed to avoid contact with enemy vessels. Several U-boat commanders later swore they had spotted the *Queen Mary* through their periscopes, only to have her quickly steam out of range. She was hunted, but never snared.

The *Queen Mary*'s wartime job was not finished at the war's end, as she shouldered the herculean task of returning war-weary American and Canadian soldiers to their homelands and families. The wounded were also returned, after the liner was fitted out as a floating hospital including surgical and intensive care units in the larger lounges and drawing rooms. Voyage after voyage, the *Queen Mary* carried the triumphant soldiers home to their wives and children after months of arduous warfare.

Following the return of the soldiers, the *Queen Mary* was conscripted into further service as another type of transport. Thousands of American and Canadian soldiers married Europeans during the war, and the brides were anxious to join their husbands. On thirteen voyages, the *Queen Mary* safely transported 22,000 war brides and children to their husbands in the United States and Canada. The ship's lounges and drawing rooms resembled giant nurseries, with diapers and baby clothes drying on makeshift clotheslines. Four new American and Canadian citizens were born on these trips.

Opposite page:
The war is over! Triumphant and excited members of the 30th Infantry Division unfurl their banner as the Queen Mary *arrives in New York.*

The Queen Mary *receives a joyous welcome in Southampton, her home port, as she returns for the first time after nearly six years of wartime service.*

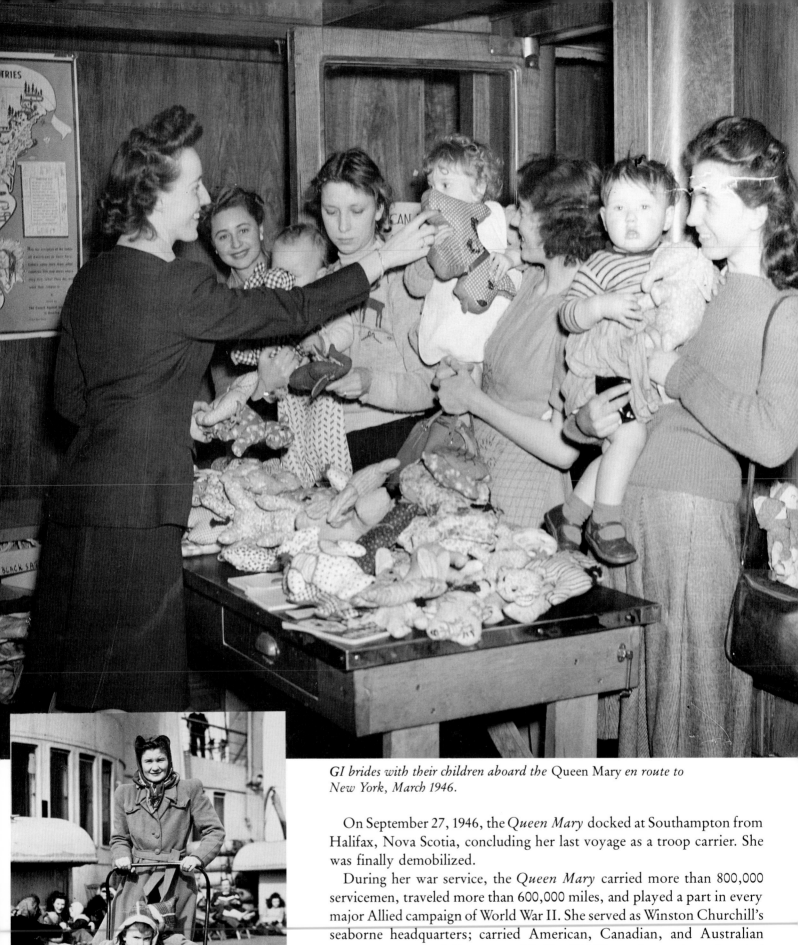

GI brides with their children aboard the Queen Mary *en route to New York, March 1946.*

On September 27, 1946, the *Queen Mary* docked at Southampton from Halifax, Nova Scotia, concluding her last voyage as a troop carrier. She was finally demobilized.

During her war service, the *Queen Mary* carried more than 800,000 servicemen, traveled more than 600,000 miles, and played a part in every major Allied campaign of World War II. She served as Winston Churchill's seaborne headquarters; carried American, Canadian, and Australian troops; transported German and Italian POWs; and served as a hospital ship and bridal transport — all without her passengers sighting or being attacked by an enemy vessel or aircraft. With all her protective armament, the *Queen Mary*'s guns were never fired during the war.

A GI bride and her children take a turn around the Sun Deck. The Queen Mary *carried more than 22,000 women and children to the United States and Canada, where they rejoined husbands and fathers.*

Bathed and powdered, a happy baby stares curiously at the photographer. The woman on the bunk puts on a little powder of her own.

Together, the *Queen Mary* and *Queen Elizabeth* had been the equal of a fleet of twenty lesser ships. Sir Winston Churchill, in his memoirs, conceded that the *Queen Mary* had been instrumental in shortening the war. Cunard Chairman Sir Percy Bates commented, "I would like to think the two ships shortened the war by one year." The *Queen Mary*, pride of Great Britain, had endeared herself to millions of American soldiers, and, indeed, the entire free world owed her a great debt of gratitude.

If the *Queen Mary* had been built just for wartime use, she would have justified her construction costs. But the liner still had a glorious future ahead of her.

The Statue of Liberty welcomes a shipload of new citizens to the United States. The brides, married to American soldiers, soon will be reunited with their husbands.

After many months of reconversion, she was ready to resume her place as Queen of the Atlantic. To restore the passenger liner to her former glory was a gargantuan task. Furniture, artwork, and other fittings were gathered from warehouses around the world and shipped to Southampton. All evidence of the years of difficult military use had to be erased from the *Queen Mary*'s lounges and cabins. Bit by bit, workmen gradually reclaimed the look of elegance and sophistication with which the *Queen Mary* had been designed and constructed.

Finally, the *Queen Mary* was ready to begin again the job for which she was created. For the next twenty years, the *Queen Mary* and her sister ship would be a moving bridge across the Atlantic, safely transporting millions of passengers between two continents now at peace.

Opposite page, top:
The Queen Mary *steams gracefully past downtown Manhattan with a full load of happy homeward-bound soldiers.*

Opposite page, bottom:
As the Queen Mary *approaches her Pier 90 berth in New York, returning troops receive a warm and well-deserved welcome.*

RETURN TO PEACETIME SERVICE:

THE QUEEN MARY LEGACY

Winston Churchill, seated in the First-Class Drawing Room, returns on the Queen Mary *from talks with President Harry Truman in 1951.*

Chapter IV

Opposite page:
High and dry, the Queen Mary
looms over the dry dock during
her annual overhaul.

On July 31, 1947, the RMS *Queen Mary* sailed from Southampton on her first peacetime voyage in nearly eight years, performing the task for which she had been built: the weekly two-ship express service to New York. The two great Queens of the Atlantic ran like clockwork — week after week, month after month — providing regular mail and passenger service. As the *Queen Mary* sailed from Southampton, the *Queen Elizabeth* departed from New York, passing each other in mid-Atlantic. In calm, clear water, the sister ships' captains charted their courses to within a few thousand feet of each other. No matter what the time when the two ships passed, night or day, hundreds of enthusiastic passengers lined the rails, waving and cheering as the two superliners swept past one another at a combined speed of more than sixty miles per hour.

On almost every voyage, the *Queen Mary* carried notable passengers; foreign dignitaries, film stars, literary greats. Great Britain's prime minister, Sir Winston Churchill, and his wife were aboard for the westbound crossing in January 1953, en route to Washington D.C. for a series of conferences with President-Elect Dwight D. Eisenhower. And in November 1954, Elizabeth, the Queen Mother, returned to England aboard the *Queen Mary*, ending a goodwill tour of America. During the voyage, the Queen Mother continued to spread good will as she visited the crew's quarters and the working areas of the ship, greeting and chatting with members of the crew.

Workmen use their brushes as paddles in the dry dock at Southampton in December 1954. The men will wash down the liner's hull as the water recedes.

*The work crews prepare the liner to
return to transatlantic passenger service
in 1947. Here, the librarian inventories
books in the Second-Class Library
while workmen reinstall fixtures.*

The weekly transatlantic crossings did not always run like clockwork. As the *Queen Mary* approached New York Harbor on February 6, 1953, Captain Donald Sorrell received the news that all of New York's tugboats were out of service due to a workers' strike. Cunard officials, hoping to maintain the ship's tight schedule, radioed Sorrell, asking if he could dock the *Queen Mary* without tugboats. Although it was only his second voyage as relief captain, Sorrell, a man with enormous confidence in his ship and his own skill, radioed back, "Certainly! I will be delighted."

It was a herculean task. Normally four or five tugboats were required to dock the *Queen Mary* in New York. Her four massive thirty-five-ton propellers were intended to power the ship at high speeds on the open sea — they were not designed to maneuver the giant liner in close quarters, where mere inches meant the difference between success and disaster.

The docking process was further complicated by the slow-moving but powerful current of the Hudson River. But, undaunted, Captain Sorrell carefully maneuvered the *Queen Mary* up the Hudson to Pier 90. Proceeding to the bridge wing, he carried with him a special sighting instrument — a crude block of wood sporting a formation of nails — he had invented for just such an emergency. He lined up the *Queen Mary* to her dock with the instrument, then slowly inched the great ship forward, cautioning the quartermaster to hold her straight and steady. A tiny lifeboat was dispatched from the nearby Cunarder *Caronia* to carry the docking lines to the pier.

As the *Queen Mary*'s bow moved past the end of the pier, it seemed Sorrell had achieved the impossible on his first attempt. But suddenly, the current of the Hudson River caught the ship's stern, edging it menacingly toward the pier. The massive bow, which had cut a light cruiser in half during World War II, swung toward the West Side Highway. At even the slowest speed, the *Queen Mary*'s weight and momentum could greatly damage the pier. Spectators crowding the dock hurriedly moved back, expecting the worst.

On the bridge, Captain Sorrell recognized the danger and calmly ordered the quartermaster, "All astern." Just in time, the ship moved back from the dock to midchannel. Sorrell decided to try again. Using the strong Hudson River current to his advantage, he moved the *Queen Mary* forward into the dock. Using the ship's lines and docking equipment, he brought the *Queen Mary* into the dock on his second attempt, calmly telling the quartermaster, "All stop. Finished with engines." The next day, Captain Sorrell's achievement was proclaimed in headlines around the world.

*During the ship's 1951 overhaul in Southampton, workmen
rehang the First-Class Main Lounge curtains after cleaning.*

Screen star Marlene Dietrich clutches her hat on the breezy Sports Deck as the Queen Mary *travels at more than thirty miles per hour.*

Only one other captain had previously docked the *Queen Mary* without the aid of tugboats. In October 1938, Commodore R. B. Irving also accomplished this amazing feat in the remarkable time of thirty-four minutes, the same docking time needed with the aid of twelve tugboats.

The postwar 1940s and the decade of the 1950s proved to be a time of prosperity for the *Queen Mary* and the *Queen Elizabeth*. Month after month, they continued the weekly transatlantic schedule, carrying full complements of contented passengers.

But with the advent of jet aircraft and improved air safety records in the 1960s, the liners' future became cloudy. While the sister ships took nearly five days, jets crossed the Atlantic in seven hours. In the era of the jet age, speed became king, and the *Queen Mary*'s passenger loads began to dwindle. By the midsixties, the *Queen Mary* carried just a fraction of her former passenger complements.

Fred Astaire pauses at a stairway for the ship's photographer.

Douglas Fairbanks, Jr. and Norma Shearer dance in the Verandah Grill.

The Duke of Windsor, formerly King Edward VIII, was a frequent passenger.

David Niven breaks into a lively Highland fling upon arrival at Southampton in July 1947. He was on his way to star in the London film production of Bonnie Prince Charlie.

Clark Gable with the ship's chief steward.

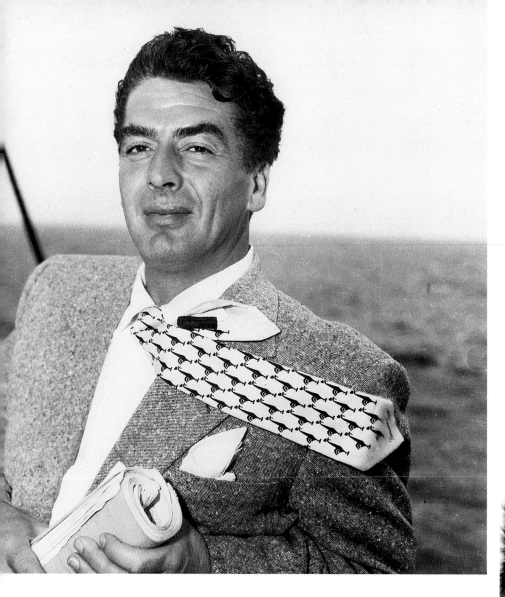

Handsome and jauntily attired Victor Mature braves a cool breeze on the liner's Sun Deck.

Glamorous Gloria Swanson strikes an alluring pose during a transatlantic crossing.

Olympic swimmer and gold medalist Johnny Weissmuller watches the horizon from the Sports Deck.

In an attempt to increase the *Queen Mary*'s revenue, Cunard reduced the frequency of Atlantic crossings and used her for a number of short cruises to various ports. The *Queen Mary* was unsuccessful as a cruise ship, however. She was too large to dock at most harbors, requiring her passengers to go ashore via small launches. Finally, in May 1967, after several years of multimillion-dollar losses, Cunard announced that both the *Queen Mary* and *Queen Elizabeth* would be sold.

Numerous proposals were put forth for the *Queen Mary*, ranging from the practical to the bizarre. Several cities, including New York, wanted to use the ship as a youth hostel or floating classroom facility. An imaginative Southern gentleman suggested welding together the *Queen Mary* and *Queen Elizabeth* to make the world's largest catamaran. But in a sealed-bid auction, the City of Long Beach, California, became the new owner of the *Queen Mary* with a bid of $3.45 million and plans to convert the ship into a floating hotel, tourist attraction, and maritime museum.

Cunard officials then met with the Long Beach delegation to discuss transporting the *Queen Mary* from England to California. Cunard proposed sailing the *Queen Mary* to Long Beach with a skeleton crew, but Long Beach officials insisted on bringing the ship home in grand style with a full complement of passengers. In fact, one of the stipulations of the bid was that the *Queen Mary* be booked for one last cruise from Southampton to Long Beach. Cunard tried to dissuade the delegation from booking a passenger cruise, but they were adamant. Reluctantly, Cunard agreed to help with the planning of the voyage.

The problems involved were tremendous. Too large to pass through the Panama Canal, the *Queen Mary* would have to sail around Cape Horn on the southernmost tip of South America. The ship would cross the equator

Seductive oriental beauty Anna May Wong relaxes in the ship's First-Class Main Lounge in 1937.

RESCUE AT SEA

The Queen Mary had many adventures during her thirty-one years at sea, but none was more exciting than a daring mid-Atlantic rescue on January 29, 1955. As the Queen Mary wallowed heavily in high seas whipped by gale-force winds, stewards served a sparsely attended afternoon tea in the Dining Salon. In the radio room, meanwhile, the operator jotted down an urgent request for help: "TWO SEAMEN FALLEN FROM TWIN DECK TO HOLD #2 STOP THEY MORTALLY WOUNDED STOP PLEASE ANY SHIP WITH DOCTOR."

Three hundred and twenty-three miles from the Queen Mary, aboard the 7,100-ton Panamanian freighter Liberator, two injured men were dying from the lack of medical assistance.

Within minutes, the Liberator's message was delivered to Captain Donald Sorrell on the bridge of the Queen Mary. Captain Sorrell quickly considered the situation. Other ships were closer to the Liberator, but the Queen Mary had two surgeons and a hospital with medical equipment. Weighing two men's lives against the economics of deviating from the ship's tight schedule, he made his decision at once. At full speed, the Queen Mary turned and raced toward the Liberator.

The Queen Mary reached the Liberator at 1:30 A.M. the following morning. With moderate-gale winds beating the sea into froth, Captain Sorrell switched on his searchlights and delicately maneuvered the massive ship into position between the smaller vessel and the screaming winds.

Senior First Officer Leslie Goodier mustered his crew and boarded the lifeboat on the Sun Deck, lowering the small craft eighty-five feet into the sea. The wind buffeted the Queen Mary's greatly exposed hull, causing her to roll heavily and making the rescue effort a dangerous operation. Huddled in the the lifeboat was the ship's junior surgeon, Dr. Timothy Yates, who volunteered to board the Liberator and attend the injured seamen.

Tossed to and fro by the towering waves, the lifeboat took eleven minutes to cross to the freighter. As the small craft slammed against the Liberator's hull, Dr. Yates leaped from the boat to cling precariously to a rope boarding ladder before being hauled aboard by the freighter's crewmen.

The lifeboat could not remain alongside the freighter in the furious seas. The craft was in danger of capsizing, and the crew was suffering from exposure. The men were forced to return to the Queen Mary, and the lifeboat was hoisted aboard the liner.

Goodier, reporting to the captain, told him, "It will be absolutely impossible to get the men off in these conditions." Acting on the senior first officer's report, the captain radioed the Liberator, "DOCTOR YATES. ARE YOU PREPARED TO STAY ABOARD?" The doctor's reply came quickly, "NO, THIS SHIP GOING TO CANADA! WE ARE READY TO LOWER PATIENTS NOW IF YOU ARE READY."

Sorrell murmured to the bridge crew, "He doesn't realize how bad it is. We'll have to send a message telling him he must stay." They all knew the injured men's chances of survival were poor if they could not be transferred to the Queen Mary's hospital.

A quiet voice broke the joyless reflection. "I think I can do it, sir, if you will let me get another volunteer crew," said the Queen Mary's chief officer, Lt. Commander Phillips A. Read. "You're quite sure?" asked the captain. "Certain," Read replied.

Read's plan required perfect timing. The captain would bring the Queen Mary as close as possible to the Liberator, holding the liner broadside to the shrieking wind to give the freighter's crew a brief lull in which to lower the wounded men into the lifeboat. It was a risky procedure. A large ship stopped in the water is difficult to maneuver. Because the exposed area of the Queen Mary's hull and superstructure was three times her underwater area, she could could move sideways, accelerating rapidly in just minutes when caught in high winds.

Read and his crew lowered the lifeboat and, as if on a roller coaster, careened through twenty-five-foot waves to the side of the Liberator. With his boat in position, Read used a signal lamp to alert the Queen Mary's captain. Acting quickly, Sorrell eased his ship alongside the freighter. The plan worked – the Liberator lay in the calm of the lee provided by the massive ocean liner.

Within minutes, Dr. Yates and the two seamen were lowered into the lifeboat. But the Queen Mary was drifting dangerously close to the Liberator, threatening to crush the much smaller vessel. The instant the lifeboat cleared the freighter's side, Captain Sorrell ordered the Queen Mary's engines full astern. The four giant screws foamed the sea as the ship knifed backward, away from the wallowing freighter – the Queen Mary's bow clearing the Liberator by only fifty feet!

As the lifeboat was hauled up the side of the Queen Mary, it swung inboard, smashing hard against the liner's hull. Read, unprepared for the impact, was hurled overboard into the churning sea. Reacting instantly, an AB (able-bodied seaman) grabbed Read's feet, yanking him back into the boat just as it lifted clear of the sea's surface.

The injured and unconscious seamen, carried to the Queen Mary's hospital where the ship's doctor's attended them, later recovered fully in a Southampton hospital.

Perhaps more than any single incident in the Queen Mary's illustrious career, this daring sea rescue illustrated that, beneath the glamour and elegance, her captain and crew were brilliant seamen, with the courage and stamina to challenge the fury of the North Atlantic.

The First-Class Dining Salon is decorated with beautiful paintings, wood carvings, and glasswork. This painting by Dame Laura Knight, entitled The Mills Circus, *is from one of the private dining rooms adjoining the main hall.*

twice, steaming into hot tropical climates for which she was not equipped, having air conditioning only in one Second-Class and six First-Class public rooms. Fuel and water difficulties were also staggering. A route had to be devised that included refueling ports large enough to accommodate her 1,019½-foot length and forty-foot-deep draught, and that were close in location to replenish her fresh water supply.

Eventually, the problems were solved, and the *Queen Mary* was ready to begin the thirty-nine-day voyage billed as her "Last Great Cruise."

Departing from Southampton, England, on October 31, 1967, the *Queen Mary* attracted worldwide attention as she commenced her last crossing, a voyage that would add many new records to her already distinguished career. Thousands of Britons turned out to wish their ship a tearful farewell. As the *Queen Mary* eased away from the dock, the ship's 310-foot-long "paying off" pennant streamed from her mainmast; each year of service represented by ten feet of colorful banner.

The beautiful mural over a fireplace in the First-Class Lounge is entitled Unicorns in Battle. *It was created by Alfred Oakley and Gilbert Bayes, and is a gesso panel — a wood carving overlaid with plaster, then decorated with gold and silver gilt.*

THE QUEEN MARY CREW

The number of crew personnel varied from voyage to voyage depending upon the number of passengers. However, although the number of catering department waiters, stewards, and attendants fluctuated, the deck and engine departments usually remained constant.

Captain: 1.
Staff Captain: 1.
Deck Department: 188 total.

Navigating Officers: 8–Chief, Senior First, Junior First, Senior Second, Junior Second, Senior Third, Intermediate Third, Junior Third.
Radio Officers: 12.
Carpenter: 1.
Assistant Carpenters: 4.
Bosun: 1.
Bosun's Mates: 3.
Master at Arms (MAA): 8.
Fire Patrol: 6.
Storekeeper: 1.
Lamp Trimmer: 1.
Quartermasters: 6.
Able-Bodied Seamen: 57.
Ordinary Seamen and Boy Seamen: 8.

- Pursers: 58 total.
  Purser: 1.
  Staff Purser: 1.
  Assistant Pursers: 20.
  Baggage Master: 3.
  Interpreter: 1.
  Printers: 5.

Musicians: 20.
Photographers: 3.
Telephone Operators: 4.

- Medical Staff: 14 total.
  Surgeons: 2.
  Nursing Sisters: 4.
  Physiotherapist: 1.
  Dispenser: 1.
  Hospital Attendants: 3.
  Officers' Stewards: 3.

Engine Department: 254 total.

Engineering Officers: 64.
Electrical Engineering Officers: 22.
Sanitary Engineer: 1.
Boiler Maker: 1.
Plumbers: 6.
Engineering Writers: 2.
Leading Hands: 3.
Storekeeper: 1.
Assistant Storekeepers: 3.
Refrigeration Attendant: 1.
Electric Greasers: 6.
Deck and Main Greasers: 45.
Firemen: 42.
Trimmers: 46.
Trimmers' Peggys: 8.
Cinema Operators: 3.

Catering Department: 829 total.

Chief Steward: 1.
Second Steward: 1
Restaurant Managers: 2.
Bedroom Stewards: 181.

Waiters, Commissary Waiters, and Trainees: 204.
Night Stewards and Assistants: 36.
Officers' Stewards: 32.
Deck and Public Room Stewards: 39.
Kitchen Staff: 158.

- Women's Staff: 73 total.
  Stewardesses: 44.
  Nursery Stewardesses: 3.
  Bath Attendants: 10.
  Shop Attendants: 7.
  Swimming Pool Attendants: 2.
  Hairdressers: 6.
  Turkish Bath Attendant: 1.

- Other Personnel: 102 total.
  Pantrymen, Bellboys, Shoeboys, Linen Storekeepers, Chief Storekeeper and Assistants, Clothes Pressers, Utilitymen, Gardeners, Writers, Lift (Elevator) Attendants, Barbers, Physical Training Instructors, Swimming Pool Attendants, Masseurs, and Turkish Bath Attendants.

Summary: 1,273 total.

Captain: 1.
Staff Captain: 1.
Deck Department: 188.
Engine Department: 254.
Catering Department: 829

The per-day cost of operating the ship was: 1936–$30,000.

1956–$56,000.   1967–$70,000.

The Royal Marine Corps Band played "Auld Lang Syne" as Royal Navy helicopters flew overhead in a giant anchor formation. Hundreds of boats and ships of all sizes swarmed about the harbor as the *Queen Mary* prepared to sail, filling the air with sounds of horns and whistles.

This "Last Great Cruise" was the ship's longest peacetime voyage — 14,559 miles — and took her to some of the world's most exotic ports: Lisbon, Portugal; Las Palmas, Canary Islands; Rio de Janeiro, Brazil; Valparaiso, Chile; Callao, Peru; Balboa, Panama; and Acapulco, Mexico.

To save fuel, only two of the ship's four engines and propellers were to be used during the voyage. But, with the rough weather and the enormous drag of the two unused propellers, it soon became apparent that the *Queen Mary* would have trouble maintaining her schedule. Her first stop at Lisbon was, in fact, delayed when the giant liner missed the high tide necessary for her safe entry into the harbor.

During the first long leg of the voyage — the 3,500-mile expanse between Las Palmas and Rio de Janeiro — some passengers complained of the heat as the ship passed through tropical waters. Most, however, remained cheerful, having been warned about the heat before booking passage.

Starting platform in the After Engine Room. A portion of two of the massive turbines is visible in the lower part of the photograph.

Opposite page:
An alert crew constantly manned the Wheelhouse, which was the command center of the huge liner.

Whenever weather permitted, the captains of the Queen Mary *and* Queen Elizabeth *steered their ships to pass as closely as possible in mid-Atlantic. As the two ships steamed toward each other at combined speeds of more than sixty miles per hour, the captains would salute each other's ship with three long blasts of their whistles.*

Hundreds of boats and thousands of spectators bid the Queen Mary *a fond farewell as the liner departs New York for the last time on September 22, 1967.*

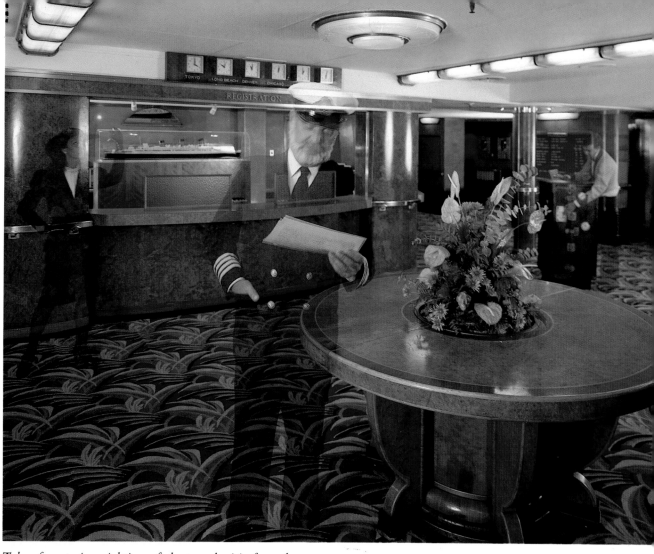

*Tales of mysterious sightings of ghosts and spirits from the
Queen Mary's sailing days continue to be told today.*

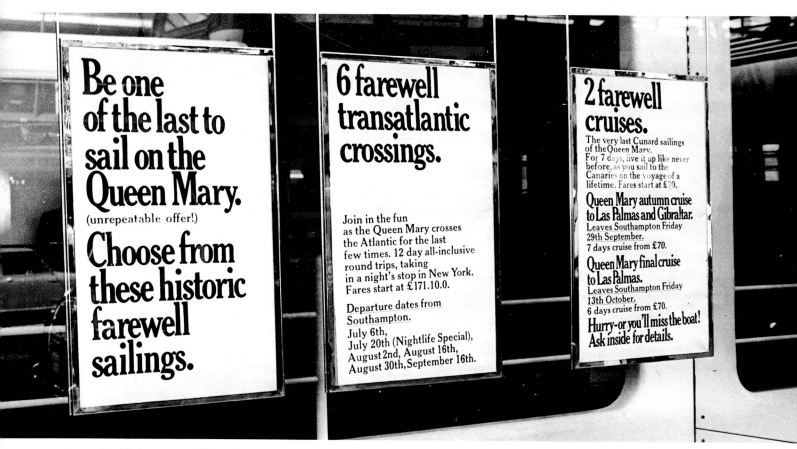

Be one of the last to sail on the Queen Mary.

(unrepeatable offer!)

Choose from these historic farewell sailings.

6 farewell transatlantic crossings.

Join in the fun
as the Queen Mary crosses
the Atlantic for the last
few times. 12 day all-inclusive
round trips, taking
in a night's stop in New York.
Fares start at £171.10.0.

**Departure dates from
Southampton.**

July 6th,
July 20th (Nightlife Special),
August 2nd, August 16th,
August 30th, September 16th.

2 farewell cruises.

The very last Cunard sailings
of the Queen Mary.
For 7 days, live it up like never
before, as you sail to the
Canaries on the voyage of a
lifetime. Fares start at £70.

**Queen Mary autumn cruise
to Las Palmas and Gibraltar.**
Leaves Southampton Friday
29th September.
7 days cruise from £70.

**Queen Mary final cruise
to Las Palmas.**
Leaves Southampton Friday
13th October.
6 days cruise from £70.

**Hurry-or you'll miss the boat!
Ask inside for details.**

*Cunard publicity posters offer a chance
to sail on the* Queen Mary's *final cruises.*

111

As the Queen Mary *leaves Southampton on her final voyage October 31, 1967, Royal Navy helicopters fly overhead in the formation of a giant anchor.*

The captain and crewmen pose on the Promenade Deck with the Queen Mary's *310-foot-long "paying off" pennant, a traditional streamer flown on a ship's last voyage. (Ten feet represented each year of service, hence the* Queen Mary's *pennant was 310 feet long for her thirty-one years of service.) Pictured from left to right are Fredrick H. Egerton, boatswain; John Treasure Jones, the* Queen Mary's *last captain; Joseph S. Allen, chief deck steward; and Robert Wilson, quartermaster.*

After a stopover in Rio de Janeiro, the *Queen Mary* prepared to round Cape Horn. Crewmen tied down everything moveable in anticipation of Cape Horn's notorious rough seas and violent storms, neither of which materialized. Hundreds of passengers, standing in the cold air, lined the decks to witness the historic moment when the *Queen Mary* rounded the cape. She was the largest ship to carry the greatest number of passengers ever around Cape Horn.

Many passengers were not content to just sail around Cape Horn. Some rode in English double-decker buses parked on Main Deck, where the two bright-red buses were lashed, on their way to Long Beach. Dr. Orville W. Cole, a Long Beach physician and the former president of the Long Beach Chamber of Commerce, sold tickets to "Ride Around the Cape" as a fundraiser. The idea was a sellout, and the money was donated to a school

RADIOGRAM

CUNARD STEAM-SHIP CO. LTD.

RADIO SERVICES OPERATED BY
INTERNATIONAL MARINE RADIO CO., LTD.

Received by R.M.S. "QUEEN MARY"   Date....24/9/67.............

Form B.52M
Printed in England

PREAMBLE:	PREFIX	OFFICE OF ORIGIN NUMBER	NO. OF WORDS	DATE	TIME	SERVICE INSTRUCTIONS		
RADIO:	MSG	QUEEN ELIZABETH	N/C	24				
TO	CAPTAIN TREASURE JONES							
						RECEIVED		
						FROM	TIME	BY
		QUEEN MARY				GBSS	1452Z	JW

YOU can telephone or telegraph to any part of the world from this ship. You can thus use the radio service to reply to this message, to reserve accommodation on shore, and make railway and aeroplane reservations from mid-ocean in advance of your arrival.

You can also communicate with your home or business at any time during the voyage.

Enquiries respecting this message should be made at the International Marine Radio Co. Ltd's Radio Office on board, or addressed to the International Marine Radio Co. Ltd., Peall Road, Croydon, Surrey, and must be accompanied by this form.

Please read on the back of this form the conditions under which this message has been transmitted.

COMMEMORATING VESSEL'S LAST VOYAGE

CHIEF RADIO OFFICE

1400Z POS 4938N 3005W CO 259 SPEED 27.5 KTS WIND NW 6 BARO 996 CLOUDY AND CLEAR WE HAD A BIT OF A BLOW YESTERDAY JUST OFF IRELAND BUT IT LOOKS AS IF THOUGH YOU SHOULD HAVE FOLLOWING WINDS .
IT IS A SAD MOMENT AS THESE TWO GREAT SHIPS PASS FOR THE LAST TIME BUT WE HOPE TO SEE YOU SHORTLY AFTER MIDNIGHT NEW TIME AND MOST OF MY PASSENGERS ARE WAITING UP FOR THIS HISTORIC EVENT HOPE THAT YOU AND YOUR WIFE ENJOY THE TRIP ROUND CAPE HORN REGARDS AND BEST WISHES

GEOFFREY

Shortly before the two great ships met for the last time at sea, Commodore Geoffrey Marr of the Queen Elizabeth *sent this radiogram to Captain John Treasure Jones of the* Queen Mary. *As the message indicates, the sister ships passed each other in the darkness after midnight on September 25, 1967.*

Steaming up the California coastline, the Queen Mary *is greeted by an aerial "welcome wagon" as a Douglas DC-9 flies over the ship and drops carnations on the upper decks. When the* Queen Mary *approached New York Harbor at the end of her maiden voyage on June 1, 1936, Eddie Rickenbacker welcomed the ship in the same manner from a DC-2.*

Map shows the route of the Queen Mary's *14,000-mile voyage from Southampton to Long Beach.*

Cunard often commissioned Bassett-Lowke, Ltd. to build models of their new liners. The model of the Queen Mary *is 1/48 the actual size of the liner (constructed on a scale of 1/4 inch to one foot). The model is twenty-one feet long and weighs more than a ton. It was constructed from a single log of 200-year-old white mahogany from Africa. The log was first cut into planks, which were then laminated together for greater strength to prevent warping and cracking. The model has more than 4,600 individual fittings on it.*

in Valparaiso, Long Beach's sister city and the *Queen Mary*'s next port.

Another enterprising passenger, Dutch Miller of Long Beach, captain of the city's lifeguards, was in the First-Class pool swimming laps as the ship rounded the cape. He claimed to be the only man ever to swim around Cape Horn.

At Valparaiso, Long Beach Mayor Edwin Wade boarded the liner for the final days of the voyage, and at Acapulco, dozens of dignitaries and news reporters embarked for the jaunt to Long Beach for the final cruise of the *Queen Mary*'s career. Passengers were filled with mixed emotions — sadness that she was ending her career, and happiness that they were able to be a part of the "Last Great Cruise."

Five-hundred miles from Long Beach, the *Queen Mary* received a special welcoming tribute. A Douglas Aircraft DC-9 jetliner flew low over the great ship, dropping thousands of carnations onto her upper decks; a re-creation of the June 1, 1936, event at which Eddie Ricken-backer showered her with flowers from his DC-2 as she entered New York Harbor on her maiden voyage.

At Long Beach, the immensely popular *Queen Mary* was greeted by a flotilla of more than 5,000 vessels including rowboats, sailboats, luxury yachts, Coast Guard cutters, fire boats, and even the nuclear cruiser USS *Long Beach*, while thousands of spectators crowded the shoreline.

On her bridge, Captain John Treasure Jones watched apprehensively as thousands of small crafts converged on the *Queen Mary*, anticipating that so many vessels maneuvering in such a small space would undoubtedly incur a collision. Jones looked at the radar scope. The vessels were so densely packed around the *Queen Mary* that instead of the normal tiny blips, it showed a solid lighted mass.

Through the maze of vessels, tugboats eased the *Queen Mary* to a Pier E berth in Long Beach Harbor. There, at 12:07 P.M., Captain Jones sadly stepped up to the bridge telegraphs and signaled, "finished with engines." The *Queen Mary*'s thirty-one years of service at sea had come to an end.

The "Last Great Cruise" was a bittersweet voyage — the passengers realized that the cruise marked the end of a glorious era in steamship travel. The Queen of the Atlantic would retire in the Pacific in a city she had never visited. But she was saved from the breaker's hammer. Long Beach was not an ending; it was the beginning of a brand-new career.

Jack and Bonita Granville Wrather were frequent travelers on the Queen Mary. In 1980, Jack Wrather's company, the Wrather Corporation, assumed management of the ship's operations to 1988. In 1993, after having been managed by Disney for four years, the Queen Mary's management responsibilities were taken on by the RMS Foundation, Inc., whose president and chief executive officer is Joseph F. Prevratil, who managed the Queen Mary during the Wrather years.

Opposite page:
Permanently berthed at Pier J in the Port of Long Beach, the Queen Mary was joined in 1983 by Howard Hughes's famous seaplane, the Spruce Goose. In 1992, the Spruce Goose left its home in the giant aluminum dome adjacent to the Queen Mary and traveled north to McMinnville, Oregon. There it will be put on exhibit at the new Evergreen AirVenture Museum, which is scheduled to open in 1995.

119

VOYAGE 1002

At the 1934 launching of the *Queen Mary*, British psychic Mabel Fortescue-Harrison predicted, "Most of this generation will be gone, including myself, when this event occurs. However, the *Queen Mary*, launched today, will know its greatest fame and popularity when she never sails another mile and never carries another *paying* passenger."

Her prophecy is coming true today in Long Beach, California, where each day thousands of eager visitors flock to board history's most famous ocean liner. They walk awestruck through her elegant public rooms and marvel at the size and power of her engines.

VOYAGE 1002

The *Queen Mary* made 1,001 Atlantic crossings during her thirty-one years of passenger service, and carried the most glamorous—and most famous—people in the world. Now you, too, can sail on the *Queen Mary*, back to her glorious heyday of transatlantic splendor. See where Winston Churchill took tea and where Fred Astaire danced. Walk the ship's decks and join in the excitement as you set sail on a voyage of discovery and imagination. Book passage on the *Queen Mary* for Voyage 1002, your own personal journey into nostalgia.

THE HOTEL

As a guest of the Hotel Queen Mary, you will occupy one of the ship's original First-Class staterooms. You can still have breakfast in bed, but the *Queen Mary*, known for her excellent cuisine, even today, also offers a choice of several outstanding on-board restaurants. Live music and dancing couples—so much a part of the *Queen Mary*'s past—still fill her cocktail lounges and public rooms.

THE SHIPWALK

No visit to the ship would be complete without a tour. The *Queen Mary*'s self-guided Shipwalk courses the giant liner's bowels for a first-hand look at the one remaining massive engine room with its two 40,000 horsepower engines, and a stop at the special enclosure allowing an underwater view of one of the ship's huge thirty-five ton propellers. Throughout the Shipwalk, special film, video, and pictorial presentations exhibit highlights of the *Queen Mary*'s illustrious career. On the upper decks, stroll the promenade upon which the world's most distinguished figures walked, and step into the opulent beauty of the First-Class Main Lounge, with its three-story-high ceiling and lustrous wood paneling.

The ship's bridge and wheelhouse, whose gleaming brass speaks of an earlier age of steamship travel, is an adventure for everyone.

Before disembarking the *Queen Mary*, visit the displays showing the differences between First-Class staterooms and Third-Class cabins. For contrast, the troopship accommodations display demonstrates the crowded conditions endured by Allied soldiers during World War II crossings.

The *Queen Mary*, once the most famous ship to go to sea and now the most famous ship to come to see.